HOW
TO HAVE A
CREATIVE
CRISIS

OTHER BOOKS BY H. NORMAN WRIGHT

Crisis Counseling
Communication: Key to Your Marriage
Making Peace with Your Past
Self-talk, Imagery, and Prayer in Counseling

H. NORMAN WRIGHT

HOW TO HAVE A CREATIVE CRISIS

KEY-WORD BOOKS

AN IMPRINT
OF
WORD BOOKS, PUBLISHER
WACO, TEXAS

A DIVISION OF
WORD INCORPORATED

How to Have a Creative Crisis

Unless otherwise indicated, Scripture quotations are from the New American Standard Bible © The Lockman Foundation, 1960, 1962, 1963, 1968, 1971, 1972, 1973, 1975, and are used by permission. Those marked NIV are from the New International Version, copyright © 1978 by the New York International Bible Society. Those marked KJV are from the King James Version; and those marked AMP are from the Amplified Bible.

Library of Congress Cataloging-in-Publication Data
Wright, H. Norman.
　How to have a creative crisis.
　1. Life change events—Psychological aspects.
2. Success.　I. Title.　II. Title: Creative crisis.
BF637.L53W75　1986　　158′.1　　86–7727
ISBN 0–8499–0540–0
ISBN 0-8499-4179-2 (KW)

Printed in the United States of America
67898 OPM 987654321

Before I was afflicted I went astray.
  but now I obey your word.
It was good for me to be afflicted
  so that I might learn your decrees.
                    Psalm 119:67, 71 NIV

Contents

Part I

Surviving a Personal Crisis

1

The Storms of Life

▽

The day broke clear and crisp. The sky was clear for miles except for a trail of wispy clouds in the distance. It was a perfect day for a family reunion to celebrate the couple's sixtieth wedding anniversary. Relatives and friends were coming from hundreds of miles around. Plans had been made in secret for months without the couple knowing what was going on. Hopes were high for this special occasion and those in charge had hoped and prayed for everything to go as scheduled. And it seemed to be happening that way.

At the appointed time the people arrived and the couple were surprised and overjoyed. As the huge crowd exchanged greetings outside on the spacious lawn, no one noticed a slight breeze which began to pick up in intensity. And then in minutes dark clouds appeared overhead unleashing at first rain and then massive hailstones. People scampered for cover leaving behind food, gifts, and all of the items needed for this time of celebration. A sudden and unexpected storm had brought their carefully made plans to a halt. The people were surprised as well as disappointed for the storm came with no warning. It was totally unexpected.

Storms are like that. Some appear out of nowhere at the "wrong time" and are totally inconvenient. They disrupt our plans and some leave devastation in their path. Life is never the same after some storms have swept through our lives.

There are other storms which do give us some warning. They appear gradually and the weather forecasters are able to give us some indication in advance. To some degree we can prepare for these if the predictions are consistent and accurate. But often they aren't and once again we find ourselves unprepared.

Some storms are so new and different we aren't sure just what to do. Southern California is not known for having tornados. We have rain, Santa Ana wind conditions, earthquakes, hot weather, but tornados—no, until a few years ago, when we experienced a full-sized twister on our own street. I wasn't home but my wife Joyce was and she experienced this strange act of nature. Working out in the yard, she felt some strange and strong winds. Realizing that something was wrong, she went inside and shut the door. But the winds continued and it seemed as though the air was being sucked out of the house by this wind. Not knowing exactly what was happening, she shut herself in one of the other rooms. About this time a neighbor turned the corner to come back to her home just in time to see the twister set down in the middle of the block and begin coming toward her. She drove her car into her garage and ran into the house just before the tornado ripped the large tree from her front yard.

We were fortunate. No homes were lost but several trees were uprooted. I guess the worst part was that this was trash day and in front of each home were several full trash cans. After the tornado hit, they were empty! Everyone in our neighborhood was amazed, surprised, and some were stunned. This just doesn't happen in our area. No one knew what to do!

Some storms are totally predictable because of the climate and seasons. People will say, "Well, it's about time for our first hurricane of the year" or "Next week we'll probably have the first snow, so we had better prepare for it."

Life is full of other kinds of storms as well. We call them crises. Some are predictable, some give us a bit of warning, and others penetrate our plans and lifestyle like an alien invader. We cannot avoid them. We have to handle them in some way without being crippled or devastated for the remainder of our lives. How do you weather your storms?

Life is full of crisis. Just listen to the news for an hour or two each evening! In fact, that is what news is made of—crisis. It's the bad news of the world, not the good news. And if you have a steady diet of this input, it can warp your perspective and attitude toward life. It can make you feel overwhelmed.

As I sat down to write this chapter, I began reflecting upon the last two weeks. What has happened in the world and in my own life? One recent crisis affected the entire world. A TWA jet with all its passengers was taken hostage and almost two weeks later the remaining hostages were released in Beirut. Night after night, hours were devoted on the newscast to this tense and volatile situation.

As the hostage crisis wound down, Southern California erupted with firestorms. And again we were inundated on the TV with hour after hour of reporting. A fire in Baldwin Hills destroyed nearly one hundred homes. The pictures showed the devastation with two charred bodies lying in the street. The same night a plane crashed onto a freeway hitting a truck and killing three people. Fire broke out and a major stretch of freeway was closed for hours.

This same week I opened the morning paper to discover that one of my former students at the seminary had been shot and killed in front of his congregation on Sunday morning. Over three hundred people had viewed this tragedy during the service and had also witnessed the gunman being shot by a police officer.

Later in the week on one day I experienced the following:

A man came in for counseling and confessed to a longstanding problem of sexually abusing his stepdaughters. This had to be reported immediately to the Child Protective Agency and law enforcement.

Right after that I received a call from the IRS with the news that a payment of $3000 had been overlooked the year before and I needed to pay that within a week.

And then, I discovered that one of my bank passbooks had been lost!

Help! That's enough for one day!

This is life in the twentieth century. We cannot escape crisis situations. What then can we do about them? That's what this book is all about. *You can learn to live through your crises. Learn from them, and move ahead in your life.*

You will be able to handle crises better if you understand what a crisis is and the potential which lies within it. Far too often people think of crises as the unusual, mostly negative, events that should be avoided. Crisis and major life transitions are the stuff of which life is made. Crises have the potential for developing Christian character.

When you experience a crisis, it seems as though everything is "on the line." Webster defines crisis as a "crucial time" and "a turning point in the course of anything." This term is often used for a person's internal response to some external hazard. When you or I experience a crisis, we are thrown off guard at first. And we temporarily lose our ability to cope.

There are three possible outcomes of a crisis: a change for the better, a change for the worse, or a return to the previous level of functioning. The word crisis is rich with meaning. The Chinese term for crisis (weiji) is made up of two symbols: one is for *despair* and the other for *opportunity*. The English word is based on the Greek (krinein) meaning to *decide*. Crisis is a time of decision, judgment, as well as a *turning point* during which there will be a change for the better or worse.

When a doctor talks about a crisis, he is talking about the moment in the course of a disease when a change for the better or worse occurs. When a counselor talks about a marital crisis, he or she is talking about the turning points when the marriage can go in either direction; it can move toward growth, enrichment, and improvement or it could move toward dissatisfaction, pain, and in some cases dissolution.

When an event throws us off balance, we are experiencing a crisis. Some people allow small events to throw them off balance. A person who is very perfectionistic and rigid would allow a small annoyance to become a crisis.

The crises that you and I experience can be the result of just one event or several. It may be a problem which is too great or overwhelming, such as the death of a child. It could be a problem which has a special significance and because of this it becomes overwhelming. It could be a problem which comes at a time of special vulnerability or at a time when one is unprepared. I'm sure you've had to handle a stopped-up sink. Usually this presents no real difficulty except for the inconvenience. But if the sink stops up when you've had the flu and little or no sleep for two nights, you feel overwhelmed. It's just the last straw.

If a problem occurs, when your coping abilities are not functioning well, or when you do not have the support or help from others that you need, you feel overwhelmed and see the event as a crisis. But a crisis is not always bad. It can become a turning point in your life for the better. Yes, it can bring danger and upset but it also carries with it opportunity for growth and change. As you try to discover a way to cope you could discover a new and better way of living. The Word of God describes many individuals in a state of crisis. Paul was one of them.

> Now Saul, still breathing threats and murder against the disciples of the Lord, went to the high priest, and asked for the letters from him to the synagogues at Damascus, so that if he found any belonging to the Way, both men and women, he might bring them bound to Jerusalem. And it came about that as he journeyed, he was approaching Damascus, and suddenly light from heaven flashed around him; and he fell to the ground, and heard a voice saying to him, "Saul, Saul, why are you persecuting Me?" And he said, "Who art Thou, Lord?" and He said, "I am Jesus whom you are persecuting, but rise, and enter the city, and it shall be told you what you must do." And the men who traveled with him stood speechless,

hearing the voice, but seeing no one. And Saul got up from
the ground, and though his eyes were open; he could see nothing; and leading him by the hand, they brought him into Damas-
cus. And he was three days without sight, and neither ate nor
drank (Acts 9:1–9).

This is one of the most famous accounts of a sudden religious
conversion and very frequently such a conversion can precipitate a crisis. It is an excellent example of some of the characteristics of a crisis. This experience affected Paul in many ways.
It affected him physically for he could not see and had to be
led by the hand into the city. He was changed spiritually for
he became a believer and changed his whole pattern of responding to Christians. He was affected mentally and emotionally
for he didn't eat or drink for three days. His conversion caused
a crisis or a turning point and in his case for the better.

Let's look now at the four elements of a crisis. When you
understand these four elements you will be taking one of
the first steps toward handling life's crises in a more positive
manner.

The first element is a *sudden upsetting event*. This can be
anything which *starts* a chain reaction of events which leads
to a crisis. A young wife who prepared for her career for seven
years now discovers she is unexpectedly pregnant. A college
senior who gave himself to basketball during school in order
to play in the professional basketball association shatters an
ankle hiking. A widower raising five preadolescent children
loses his job in a very specialized profession. All of these people
have much in common. Whenever you find yourself becoming
upset or having difficulty coping, ask, "What event is occurring
or has occurred?" Identify the cause. Usually it's pretty obvious.

The second element of a crisis is *your vulnerable state*. Not
all events lead to a crisis. You have to be vulnerable in some
way for a crisis to occur. If you go without sleep for two nights,
you could be vulnerable to a situation which you usually handle
with no difficulty. Being ill or depressed lowers one's coping
ability.

Recently, I talked with a woman who wanted to give up her foster child, cancel an important fund-raising event, and quit her business. Why? Because she was depressed over the threat of another loss in her life. Thus she felt like giving up everything! I asked her not to make any decisions during her time of depression since this was not a good time to make life-changing decisions which she might regret later on.

The third element in a crisis is the *actual precipitating factor*—the last straw! These are the times when you handle one upsetting event after another very well and then go to pieces when you drop a piece of food on your clothes. Your reaction at this time is not just to the dropped food but to all of the other events.

The last element is the *state of crisis*. When you feel that you can no longer handle what is occurring, then the crisis develops. And there are several indications of this state.

Indications of a State of Crisis

Everyone differs in the way they handle a crisis. If I were to ask how you respond, what would you say?

Usually there are actual *symptoms of stress* which include physiological or psychological factors—or both. These can include depression, anxiety, headaches, bleeding ulcers, and so on. There is always some type of extreme discomfort. We all develop our own channels through which the discomfort can flow.

During this time there is also an *attitude of panic or defeat*. You may feel as though you have tried everything and nothing works. You feel like a failure, defeated, overwhelmed, and helpless. Hope? There is no hope. The whole thing is hopeless! At this point there are two ways you can respond: one is to become agitated and engage in behavior which is actually unproductive, pacing back and forth, taking drugs, driving too fast, getting into arguments or fights. The other way to respond is to become apathetic. This could include excessive sleeping or drinking to the extent that you no longer feel the pain.

17

Our main concern at this time is getting *relief.* "Get me out of this situation" is our concern and cry. We want relief from the pain of the stress. In a major crisis we are not usually in a condition to solve our problems in a rational manner. And this adds to our state of confusion because we realize we usually are capable of functioning well. A person may appear dazed or tend to respond in bizarre ways. He may feel frantic and look to other people for help. In fact, one may become very dependent upon others to help him out of the dilemma.

This is also a time of *lowered efficiency.* We may continue to function normally but instead of responding at 100 percent, our response may be at about 60 percent. This disturbs us too. The greater the threat from our appraisal of what is happening, the less effectively we will be able to cope.

Let's think about this word "appraisal" for a moment. The appraisal is what people "make" of an event. It is your own perception that this event is threatening. Some events would be threatening for everyone whereas some would be threatening just for you. Your beliefs, ideas, expectations, and perceptions all come together at this time to evaluate a situation as a crisis or a non-crisis.

Each of us has his own way of perceiving an event. If a friend of yours responds to an event differently from you, remember that it may have more meaning for him or her than it does for you. The death of a close friend is appraised from several different points of view: how close the relationship was, how often you were in touch with that friend, how you have responded to other losses, and how many losses you have experienced recently. A widow deeply involved in her husband's life perceives her loss differently than does a close friend, a business associate, or the uncle her husband saw once every five years.

When you experience a true crisis, you are perceiving the loss or threatened loss of something which is important to you. What is there at the present time in your life which could create a crisis? What is most important and significant to you?

I use the following activities to help people discover the importance of life at home.

> You have been informed that your house is going to be completely destroyed in ten minutes. You have time to make two trips out of your home taking with you what is most important and valuable to you. What will you take with you?

People are often surprised at what has meaning for them and what doesn't. It also causes them to reevaluate what they feel is important.

Another question to consider is:

> What one event, were it to occur to you in the next twelve months, would be the most upsetting or devastating to you? Now list the next four events in order of importance using the same criteria. Then think about how you would handle those events and work through the loss involved in each one.

Do you realize that even a job promotion can bring a sense of loss which precipitates a crisis? Ralph, for example, was a man who experienced such a crisis. He was a car salesman who really enjoyed the camaraderie with the other salesmen in the car agency. Then he was promoted to sales manager. This gave him more status, more money, and more changes in his relationships. He no longer was on the same level as the other salesmen and now had to push and urge them to make their sales quotas. He was very uncomfortable in this role and became so dissatisfied he began to call in sick to avoid the pressure and conflicts.

Is it possible to avoid experiencing a crisis? Not really, for crises are a definite part of our lives. But there are three factors that do affect the intensity of a crisis and may even contribute to an event becoming a crisis. One is your perception—the way you view a problem and the meaning it has for you. For example, if your daughter gets a divorce, you might see it as the greatest tragedy you could ever experience and interpret it as a commentary on your ability to raise your daughter. But other parents might not feel this way at all.

A second factor is having an adequate network of friends, relatives, or agencies that can give you support during a crisis. This is where the body of Christ should come into play as one of the greatest support groups available. But the church needs to know how to respond at such a time.

A third factor which helps determine whether an event becomes a crisis or not involves the coping mechanisms upon which most of us lean. If your coping mechanisms do not function well or break down quickly, then a crisis is inevitable. Coping mechanisms run the gamut from rationalization, denial, finding new information in a book, praying, reading scripture, and so on. Here is a fact to consider: the greater the number and diversity of coping methods, the less likely it is that a problem or upset will become a crisis.

Responding to a Crisis

When you experience a crisis, your response may differ from that of your family or friends. Are you aware of what you need or look for during a crisis? Let's look at some of the typical responses and try to identify how you respond.

Some individuals look for others to protect and control them at a time of crisis. They say, "Please take over for me."

Some need a person who will help them maintain contact with what is real and what isn't. They say, "Help me know that I am real at this time. Help me know what is going on right now."

Some feel terribly empty and need loving. They say, "Care for me. Love me."

Some need another person to be available at all times in order to feel secure. They say, "Always be there. Never leave."

Some have an urgent need to talk. They say, "Let me get this off my chest. Listen to me again and again."

Some need advice on certain pressing matters. They say, "Tell me what to do."

Some need to sort out their conflicting ideas. They say, "Help me put things into perspective."

Some need the assistance of some type of specialist. They say, "I need some professional advice."

Perhaps you identify with some of these responses. If so, why not share with those closest to you what you will probably need from them if you do experience a crisis? It will help them feel more in control and keep them from feeling overwhelmed.

Why do some people seem to handle crisis well while others struggle and flounder? Here are some of the characteristics of those who appear to have the most difficulty handling a crisis.

Some individuals are emotionally weak to begin with and thus specific events are more difficult for them to handle. Those who have a physical ailment or illness will struggle because they have less resources to draw on. Those who deny reality have a hard time coping with a crisis. Some may deny the fact they are seriously ill, or financially ruined, or that their child is on drugs or has a terminal illness.

A Harvard psychiatrist, Dr. Ralph Hirschowitz, has created a term for the next characteristic. He calls it "magic of the mouth": the tendency to eat, drink, smoke, and talk excessively. When difficulty enters these people's lives, they seem to regress into infantile forms of behavior and their mouth takes over in one way or another. They are uncomfortable unless they are doing something with their mouths most of the time. This refusal to face the real problem can continue after the crisis is over. The person is actually helping to create an additional crisis for himself.

Another characteristic is an unrealistic approach to time. Some people crowd the time dimensions of a problem or they extend the time factors way into the future. They want the problem to be "fixed" right away or they delay and delay. Delaying avoids the discomfort of a reality but enlarges the problem.

People who struggle with excessive guilt will have difficulty coping with a crisis. They will tend to blame themselves for the difficulty and by feeling worse will immobilize themselves even more.

Blamers have a difficult time coping with a crisis. They do not focus on what the problem is but turn to "who caused the problem." Their approach is to find some enemies, either real or imagined, and project the blame upon them.

A further characteristic of those who do not cope well is the tendency to be either very dependent or very independent. Such people either turn away from offers of help or become a clinging vine. Those who cling tend to suffocate you if you are involved in helping them. Overly independent people shun offers of help and even if they are sliding down the hill toward disaster they do not cry out for assistance. When the disaster hits they either continue to deny it or blame others for its occurring.

One other characteristic must be cited which has a bearing upon the others. A person's theology will affect how he or she copes with a crisis. Our lives are based upon our theology and yet so many people are frightened by the word. Our belief in God and how we perceive God is a reflection of our theology. Those who believe in the sovereignty and caring nature of God have a better basis upon which to approach life.[1]

A book which has spoken to me each and every time I have read it is Lewis Smedes' *How Can It Be All Right When Everything Is All Wrong?* His insights and sensitivity to life's crises and God's presence and involvement in our lives can answer many of our questions. He is a man who has been through life's tough times. One of his own personal experiences describes how our theology helps us move through life's changes.

> The other night, trying to sleep, I amused myself by trying to recall the most happy moments of my life. I let my mind skip and dance where it was led. I thought of leaping down from a rafter in a barn, down into a deep loft of sweet, newly mown hay. That was a superbly happy moment. But somehow

my mind was also seduced to a scene some years ago that, as I recall it, must have been the most painful of my life. Our first born child was torn from our hands by what felt to me like a capricious deity I did not want to call God. I felt ripped off by a cosmic con-artist. And for a little while, I thought I might not easily ever smile again.

But then, I do not know how, in some miraculous shift in my perspective, a strange and inexpressible sense came to be that my life, our lives, were still good, that life is good because it is *given,* and that its possibilities were still incalculable. Down into the gaps of feeling left over from the pain came a sense of *givenness* that nothing explains. It can only be *felt* as a gift of grace. An irrepressible impulse of blessing came from my heart to God for his sweet gift. And that was joy . . . in spite of pain. Looking back, it seems to me now that I have never again known so sharp, so severe, so saving a sense of gratitude and so deep a joy, or so honest.[2]

Chuck Swindoll always shares so realistically and helpfully about life's crises.

Crisis crushes. And in crushing, it often refines and purifies. You may be discouraged today because the crushing has not yet led to a surrender. I've stood beside too many of the dying, ministered to too many of the broken and bruised to believe that crushing is an end in itself. Unfortunately however it usually takes the brutal blows of affliction to soften and penetrate hard hearts. Even though such blows often seem unfair.

Remember Alexander Solzhenitsyn's admission:

It was only when I lay there on rotting prison straw that I sensed within myself the first stirring of good. Gradually, it was disclosed to me that the line separating good and evil passes, not through states, nor between classes, nor between political parties either, but right through all human hearts. So, bless you, prison, for having been in my life.

Those words provide a perfect illustration of the psalmist's instruction:

> Before I was afflicted I went astray,
> but now I obey your word.
> It was good for me to be afflicted
> so that I might learn your decrees.
> (Psalm 119:67, 71 NIV)

After crises crush sufficiently, God steps in to comfort and teach. [3]

2

The Stages of a Crisis or "Am I Normal?"

▽

You open your eyes, but you still can't see clearly. You blink and then blink again. Everything is still hazy as though you were in a thick fog. There is a sense of unreality in everything around you. You feel as though you have been run over by a three-ton truck or someone has slammed you over the head with a two-by-four. You blink again but your view of the world is still a bit fuzzy. What has happened? Are you losing your mind? Were you in an accident? Did someone hit you? Probably none of the above.

Welcome to the world of experiencing a crisis! Yes, when you and I enter into that state called "crisis time" we feel as though we have grabbed hold of a wire filled with electricity and are we ever jolted!

The Impact Phase

This is the stage of a crisis called the *impact phase*.[1] People vary in their intensity of response to a crisis but all of us feel the impact. You know immediately that something drastic has happened. You're stunned.

The impact phase is usually brief, lasting from a few hours to a few days depending upon the event and the person involved. Some impact phases linger on and on, such as in the case of a divorce proceeding.

Keep this principle in mind for yourself and for others to whom you may need to minister! The more severe the crisis (or loss), the greater the impact and the greater the amount of incapacitation and numbness. Tears might be expressed immediately or later on.

During this phase, one of the questions you must answer is, "Should I stay and face the problem or withdraw and run from it?" This is called the fight or flight pattern. A few years back, there appeared a commercial in which the person said, "I'd rather fight than switch." But not everyone feels that way in a crisis. If your tendency in the past has been to face problems, you will probably face your crisis head on. But if your tendency has been to avoid or withdraw from problems, you will probably run from your next crisis. If the crisis is especially severe, you may feel like running anyway since during the impact phase you are less competent than usual.

Facing a crisis and fighting to regain control seems to be the healthier response. Most of the time, running from a crisis is not a solution since it merely prolongs the situation. And since there are three more phases of a crisis yet to come before balance is restored, why linger? Why prolong the pain?

During the impact stage, don't expect to do any clear thinking. You will feel numb and disoriented. You may even feel as though you can't think or feel at all. Someone described it as "I feel as though my entire system shut down." Your ability to have insight is limited and you shouldn't expect to have that ability now. If a friend or family member attempts to share any factual information with you, it goes sailing right over your head. You may ask, "What did you say?" after the person has repeated it for the third time. Don't despair when this happens for this is a normal response that we all experience.

Decisions which you make at this time may be unwise but

unfortunately you may need to make some anyway. Be sure to ask a competent friend to help you.

At the heart of most crisis is a loss of some kind. Losses threaten our security, our sense of stability, and our well-being. Our self-image may be affected and there is the feeling of being out of control. The more sudden the loss, the more out of control you will feel. A gradual loss, although painful, can be prepared for to some degree. But a sudden, unexpected death may disrupt our ability to activate the emotional resources which we need to cope.

One of the most difficult types of losses to deal with is the threatened loss. For some, it is like a crisis waiting to happen. The loss has not yet occurred but there is a real possibility that it will happen. Waiting for the results of a biopsy or a state counselor's exam, or waiting to hear from the admissions office of a medical school after preparing for four years, all carry the possibility of loss.

Any kind of a loss has a way of changing our lives in a dramatic way. Even our thinking about the future is affected. The changes which occur can be positive and eventually enrich our lives. But during the first few months of a crisis, it does not feel that way to us at all. If someone were to tell you at the time of a loss that you can learn and grow when you experience a loss, you might react with disgust or anger. You aren't ready to handle thoughts like that. You need to hear such comments when life is fairly stable.

During the impact phase, in some way or another, we begin to search for what we've lost. Our thought life is focusing upon the loss. It is normal to search for something which meant a great deal to us. We are trying to hold onto our emotional attachments for a bit longer. We try to recapture the lost dream, the loved one, or even our health. The more insight we have at this time, the less we search and the less insight, the more we search!

This searching behavior often takes the form of reminiscing. How much you reminisce is in proportion to the value of what you lost. It is common (and healthy) for a person who loses

27

a loved one in death to take out photographs and other items which remind him or her of the person who died.

Recently I was counseling a young woman who had lost her father six months before. She had flown back east for the funeral but had not gone back since. This meant that she had not had the opportunity to spend time in the home where her father lived or to reminisce with friends or other relatives. Because of this, her grief was blocked. I suggested that she write her mother and ask her to send the photograph album which contained the pictures of her and her father. When it arrived, I encouraged her to sit down with a friend and look through the book, telling about the various experiences each picture portrayed. We need to reminisce.

It is normal and healthy to express as many feelings as you can. And you need someone to listen to you and accept those feelings. Avoid those people who try to make you stifle your feelings. Feelings should not be buried or denied at this point for feelings rejected delay the resolution of the problem. When feelings are buried, they are frozen.

Do you know what happens to water when it is frozen? The molecules actually expand. Thus water frozen in pipes has the power to burst those steel pipes wide open. Frozen emotions take on a power out of proportion to their original nature. When we lock up a summer mountain cabin for the winter, it is important to drain all of the water from the pipes if we want them to function properly the next spring. During grief and crisis, it is important to keep the channels open for the feelings to flow when they need to.

Some of us use verbal expression to release our feelings because that is what we know best. But others find other means to empty themselves of their emotions. We shouldn't compare ourselves with others and say one way of release is the only way or the best way. Some people talk about their hurt and grief and some act it out. You may have a friend who spends a great deal of time working in the yard or running but does not talk about the loss of her spouse. You may be concerned that she is not dealing with her loss, but she may be doing just that in her own way.

For some, rigorous physical activity can bring about the healing and there are many unique responses that people express to cope with their loss. I heard of a man who had lost his father in a tragic fire. He lived near his father on an adjacent farm. One night the home in which he was born and raised burned to the ground with his father inside. His response to this tragedy startled other family members. He remained silent while they all wept and talked about the loss. This man borrowed a bulldozer and proceeded to bulldoze the ashes and charred remains of the house.

The rain had stopped the fire and this was his own expression of burying his father. He worked for hours, not even stopping for meals or rest. When darkness came, he continued ignoring the requests of family members to stop for the night. He continued to bulldoze the remains back and forth, again and again.

This man and his father were farmers and for most of their lives had worked together in the fields. They didn't verbalize very much together nor share feelings. But theirs was a close, nonverbal relationship.

You and I may grieve with tears but he grieved with his borrowed bulldozer. This was his own personal expression of words and tears. He cried by working the land over and over again until nothing was visible. He gave his father and the home a proper burial but in his own way. The land, which in a sense was his father's cemetery, was now ready to be farmed and it would be by him. If you were to ask this man why he had done this, he could not give you an answer. He didn't know why but he did something with his grief and it was probably the best thing he could have done.[2]

What do you need during the impact phase of a crisis? You need to accept your feelings. You need an environment which helps your grieving and hurts to heal. Avoid those people who are full of advice and who say, "I told you so," or "Spiritual Christians get over their hurt sooner than others."

Find the accepting people and those who know how to minister to you during a crisis. The people who can help you most are empathetic.

They don't shock easily but accept your human feelings.

They are not embarrassed by your tears.

They do not give unwanted advice.

They are warm and affectionate with you according to your needs.

They help you recall your strengths when you have forgotten you have strengths.

They trust you to be able to come through this difficult time.

They treat you like an adult who can make your own decision.

They may become angry with you but do not attack your character.

They respect your courage and sense of determination.

They understand that grief is normal and they understand the stages of grief.

They too may have been through times of difficulty and can share those times with you.

They try to understand what your feelings mean to you.

They are faithful to commitments and promises.

They pray with you and for you.

They do not spiritualize everything.

They are sensitive to where you are spiritually and do not try to force feed you theology and scripture.[3]

Find these people and cultivate their friendship before a crisis hits. But remember that we draw those kinds of people to us as we demonstrate that we are the same kind of person.

Let's summarize now what happens to you during the impact phase. This phase will take a few hours to a few days. You will either want to face and fight the situation or flee from it. Your thinking will be somewhat numb and disoriented. You will search for whatever it is that you have lost, often by reminiscing. And you need people to accept your feelings.

Why am I telling you about these phases of a crisis?

1. By knowing what the four phases of a crisis are you will realize that you are not going crazy, you are going through a normal passage.

2. By becoming aware of these phases now, some of the pain and pressure may be relieved later on. You can recall, "Oh, yes, this phase will pass and I will go into the next one."

3. You will realize there is light at the end of the tunnel. There is hope.

4. And perhaps you can gain control of your life and the outcome a bit sooner by knowing what to expect.

As Ann Stearns puts it:

> Recovery from loss is like having to get off the main highway every so many miles because the direct route is under reconstruction. The road signs reroute you through little towns you hadn't expected to visit and over bumpy roads you hadn't wanted to bounce around on. You are basically traveling in the appropriate direction. On the map, however, the course you are following has the look of shark's teeth instead of a straight line. Although you are gradually getting there, you sometimes doubt that you will ever meet up with the finished highway.[4]

The Withdrawal-Confusion Phase

After the impact phase you will move into the *withdrawal-confusion phase*. This will last for days and you will feel emotionally drained. You are worn out emotionally.

During this phase the tendency to deny your feelings is probably stronger than at any other time. One reason is that your feelings now can become the ugliest. And one emotion triggers another. You may feel intense anger at whatever has occurred which in some cases brings on guilt for having such feelings. Then you feel shame and the pain from these varied responses makes the desire to repress them very strong. If some of your feelings shock others, you may want even more to repress them.

Your thinking pattern at this time will reflect a certain amount of uncertainty and ambiguity. You just aren't sure what to think or do.

During the withdrawal-confusion phase the direction of your life will become a combination of bargaining and detachment. Bargaining involves wishful thinking. If only this hadn't happened. If only I could recapture what I had. Perhaps there is some way to bring back what I had. This type of approach then moves to the detachment level. You need to detach yourself from whatever it was that you lost—whether it be a job, a friend, a spouse, or whatever. A widower cannot stay married to a deceased wife. An expelled student can no longer be a student in that school. A worker cannot fulfill a job he or she has lost.

During this time, you may find yourself vacillating between performing some tasks which need to be done and then reflecting and reminiscing upon how things used to be. You may feel anger at having to give up what you lost whether it be a person, an object, or an identity. We try to protect ourselves from the emptiness which loss brings. In our attempt to restore the part of us that has been lost, we will tend to distort and glorify the past. We do this to help us face the future. As we reach out to new tasks and even new people we will be doing this in an attempt to fill the void in our lives and to put something new into them.

During this time you need the assistance of caring friends and relatives to help you organize your life. You will find that you need assistance in planning your day, arranging appointments, keeping the house or job in order, and so on. Do not become hard on yourself for this apparent defect in your life since this is a normal transition which needs to be passed through. If this is a grief because of the loss of a spouse, this is not the time to be looking for another partner. It is a time to adjust.

To summarize, in the withdrawal-confusion phase (which will last for days), remember that your response will be emotional. You may feel anger, fear, guilt, rage. Your thinking process will be ambiguous and uncertain. You will vacillate from bargaining to working on detaching yourself from the lost person or situation. And during this time of puzzled searching for a way out of the difficulty, you need some task-oriented support and help from others.

The Adjustment Phase

The third phase is called the *adjustment phase.* This will take weeks to work through and the emotional responses you experience during this time are hopeful. Yes, some depression may come and go but your positive attitudes have started to form. You may begin to talk about the future with hope such as enjoying a new job, a new location, rebuilding a fire-destroyed home, considering a remarriage, and so on. You have now just about completed your detachment from what you lost. You are looking around for something new to bring into your life to which you can develop an attachment.

What happens now has started to take on some special significance for you. You have been in and through the depths of the valley and you are now climbing up the side of the mountain. Be prepared for the opinions and advice of others and sift through what you hear. Others may not see the value of what you are doing now. They may feel that you are making a drastic mistake in this new step.

Do not make any of your decisions during your down times. Wait until there is hope. And don't despair because your feelings fluctuate. Your insight is returning and your objectivity can help you process information and new suggestions. The Bible and its teaching can assist you in your decisions during this phase. You are more receptive and capable of dealing with spiritual insights. Prior to this, scripture and prayer resources were there to support and sustain you. Now is the time to seek definite answers and direction through the teaching and reading of the Word.

To summarize this phase, *remember:* It will take weeks; your positive thinking has started; you are involved in problem solving; you are searching for something new in your life;

and the best kind of support you need at this time is spiritual guidance.

The Reconstruction-Reconciliation Phase

The last period (which can take months) is the *reconstruction-reconciliation phase.* A key element here is the spontaneous expression of hope. Your sense of confidence has returned and you can now make plans again. You are able to make the conscious decision not to engage in self-pity any more. Self-initiative for new progress and reattachments are occurring. In existence now are new places, new activities, new people, new jobs, and new spiritual insights. If any of your anger and blame created difficulty during this crisis, now is the time for reconciliation.

A sign of the resolution of a crisis is the newness of a person. A crisis is an opportunity for you to gain new strengths, new perspectives on life, new appreciations, new values, and a new way to approach your life. You will look at life differently and—hopefully—not take it for granted. I know. I have been through several crises and have experienced all four phases. Sometimes it is possible to work through the four phases in less time than indicated. And sometimes one or two of the phases may take less time because of the experienced or threatened loss.

Not too long ago, I experienced some strange physical symptoms—vertigo, pressure in the back of my head, and headaches. These symptoms persisted for about seven weeks during which time the doctors had some theories but nothing concrete. Their uncertainty and my own concerns and worries about what might be wrong added to some of the feelings which I experienced. Authorities say that fear is at the heart of a crisis and that is true. If we aren't careful we can allow fear to take over and dominate and influence all of our thinking.

When my symptoms persisted, I finally went through a further examination including a CAT scan. Then the symptoms disappeared. As we attempted to piece together what had happened we felt the symptoms were there because of too many strenuous seminars with no recuperation time in between, coupled with a cold and some altitude changes. Physical exhaustion was one of the greatest culprits. But this experience at the age of 47 caused me to think, reevaluate, and make some changes. A newness occurred. I did not necessarily like what I went through but I grew because of it and feel it was necessary. I hope I will stay a bit different because of what took place.

Crisis is a part of life. But the recovery process is predictable. The chart below summarizes what I have been describing.[5]

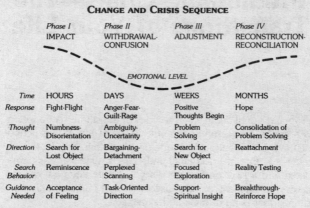

CHANGE AND CRISIS SEQUENCE

	Phase I IMPACT	Phase II WITHDRAWAL-CONFUSION	Phase III ADJUSTMENT	Phase IV RECONSTRUCTION-RECONCILIATION
Time	HOURS	DAYS	WEEKS	MONTHS
Response	Fight-Flight	Anger-Fear-Guilt-Rage	Positive Thoughts Begin	Hope
Thought	Numbness-Disorientation	Ambiguity-Uncertainty	Problem Solving	Consolidation of Problem Solving
Direction	Search for Lost Object	Bargaining-Detachment	Search for New Object	Reattachment
Search Behavior	Reminiscence	Perplexed Scanning	Focused Exploration	Reality Testing
Guidance Needed	Acceptance of Feeling	Task-Oriented Direction	Support-Spiritual Insight	Breakthrough-Reinforce Hope

When you find yourself (or someone else) experiencing a crisis, look at this chart. It will help remind you that your feelings are normal and there is hope at the end of the tunnel. Remember, too, that a crisis is an opportunity! It is a time for change and growth. There is one factor which causes a major crisis to become a growth-producing experience instead of a restrictive, crippling, eternal tragedy. That is our attitude. If our attitude has been built upon the teachings of the Word of God, that is our hope in the midst of an upset world! Our world is unstable. It rocks our boat. We are unstable. We rock our boat. But our stability comes from allowing Jesus Christ to be our rock. Isaiah 33:6, "And He shall be the stability of your times."

3

Predictable Crisis—The Transitions of Your Life

▽

From birth until death, life is a series of transitions. A transition is a bridge between two different stages of life. It is a period of moving from one state of certainty to another. But in between there is a time of uncertainty and change. One stage is terminated and a new one begun. As you know, any new change carries an element of risk, insecurity, and vulnerability, even change that is predictable and expected.

Each transition in the journey of life has the *potential* for becoming a crisis. Notice that I said the potential. A transition does not have to become a crisis. Where are you in the journey of life? Where have you been and how have you handled those changes?

For most individuals there is the transition from being single to being married, from the twenties to the thirties, the thirties to the forties, from being a couple to being parents, from being parents to the empty nest, from the empty nest to becoming grandparents, from being employed to retirement, and so on. These are all fairly predictable and can be planned for to reduce the adjustment.

But most people do not plan adequately and the new stage of life creeps up on them unaware. All of a sudden they feel carried away by a flood, totally out of control. And to make matters a bit more tense there can be those unexpected events which occur in the midst of the predictable changes such as miscarriage, marital separation and divorce, illness, disability, death of a loved one, loss of a job, relocation of the household, parents coming to live with you, an adolescent running away or using drugs, an automobile accident, fire in the home, changes in socio-economic status, and tornados. The list never ends.

Sometimes we take on additional, unexpected new roles such as becoming a part-time student while continuing as a homemaker or full-time employee, or becoming a foster parent while still parenting our own children. We may even exchange one significant role for another. You graduate from school and now instead of being a full-time student, you are a full-time employee. You experience a divorce and must give up a spouse.

Look further with me at the impact of sudden, abrupt, unpredictable changes. Listed here is a series of potentially life changing events. I would like you to rank them in order of importance or "upsetting potential" were they to occur in your life. Choose the six most upsetting events and then list them in order.

> Major illness in the family
> Jail sentence
> Unfaithful spouse
> Being fired
> Miscarriage or stillbirth
> Divorce
> Unwanted pregnancy
> Court appearance
> Death of a child
> Death of a spouse
> Major financial difficulty
> Business failure
> Marital separation due to an argument

> Unemployment for a month
> Taking out a large loan
> Broken engagement
> Academic failure
> Child married without family approval
> Lawsuit
> Loss of personally valued objects
> Death of a close friend
> Demotion
> Major personal illness
> Start of an extramarital affair

Now let's compare your list with a 1971 study by Eugene S. Pakyel in which 373 people were asked to rate the most "upsetting" events in their lives. The results of that study listed from most stressful to least stressful.[1]

1. Death of a child
2. Death of a spouse
3. Jail sentence
4. Unfaithful spouse
5. Major financial difficulty
6. Business failure
7. Being fired
8. Miscarriage or still birth
9. Divorce
10. Marital separation due to an argument
11. Court appearance
12. Unwanted pregnancy
13. Major illness in the family
14. Unemployment for a month (additional studies indicated that four out of five marriages end in divorce when the husband is out of work for nine months or more)
15. Death of a close friend
16. Demotion
17. Major personal illness
18. Start of an extramarital affair
19. Loss of personally valued objects
20. Lawsuit

21. Academic failure
22. Child married without family approval
23. Broken engagement
24. Taking out a large loan

Many changes can be planned for in advance and their intensity can be lessened. Sudden changes, however, can throw us—a person loses his job, a promotion falls through, a spouse becomes ill, a child is born with a defect, a death occurs in the family, a parent moves in.

According to family service experts,

> Any sudden change becomes a threat to whatever marital balance has been achieved. It tends to reawaken personal insecurities that the marriage has successfully overcome or held in check. You've noticed how sick people tend to fall back into childish ways—they become terribly dependent, demanding, unreasonable. Similarly, some people regress in other kinds of emotional crises. Long-conquered patterns of behavior reassert themselves, at least until the first impact of the shock has been absorbed.[2]

Predictable transitions do not have to become major storms in our lives. We don't need a satellite weather picture to tell us they are coming. Just consider your age and what stage you and your family are in. What is the next event looming close on your horizon? You can prepare for it and even rehearse mentally what you will do when those events occur. And you can gather new information to assist in the transition process.

A teacher who realized he would have to retire in ten years determined to expand his interests. He began to take courses at the local college in subjects he thought he might have an interest in. He took up photography and began reading in areas he had never considered before. He also began developing a list of projects he would like to tackle, health and finances permitting, upon retirement. Since there would be a significant loss in his life—his job and his livelihood—he planned in advance for a variety of replacements and worked through some of those feelings of loss. He also had the foresight to develop hobbies which could be enjoyed whether his health was good or poor. By anticipating what was to come he eliminated the possibility of the transition becoming a crisis. That is very important because studies indicate that many men have a serious and often unsuccessful adjustment when they retire. Depression hits many men and the suicide rate more than doubles for men over the age of sixty-five!

If moving through the various stages of life went smoothly and everything was predictable, life would be fairly easy for most mature individuals. But two factors must be considered. First of all, many of us are not yet mature nor able to take responsibility because we are stuck in our own development at an earlier stage. We may be thirty or thirty-five but only twenty emotionally. And secondly, as I mentioned earlier, some changes either come in like sudden invaders or do not occur in the time sequence which we have planned.

Some roles in life are not replaced by other duties so there is a void, such as retiring from work without finding a fulfilling task in retirement, or losing a spouse without remarrying.

There are also physical changes such as loss of one's hearing, being confined to a wheelchair for years and then regaining the ability to work, from being thin to becoming obese.

Transitions can be swift or gradual and may have either a positive or a devastating impact upon our lives.

Most people have heard of the phrase "male mid-life crisis." But did you know that only a minority of men experience a full blown mid-life crisis? And that this crisis is not inevitable? All men do go through mid-life transition which is a normal change. But we can fairly accurately predict the man who is a candidate for a full-blown crisis. He is the person who:

1. Builds his sense of identity upon his work or occupation and this is the source of meaning in his life.

2. Is out of touch with his emotions or feelings and has not learned to accept and express them.

3. Has not learned to establish close intimate friendships with other men.

Now, this is a simplified evaluation but it does hold true for most men. A man does not have to go through this crisis which in most cases creates a crisis for his family and fellow workers as well. He does have a choice.

I mentioned that another element which can throw us is the timing of some changes. This is one of the strongest determinants of a transition becoming a crisis. Each of us has our own time table. In premarital counseling I ask couples when they plan to become parents, graduate from school, move to the level of management in their career, and so on. Many have a precise time table. Most individuals have their own expectations for when certain events will occur. And some have a "mental clock" which tells them whether they are "on time" or "off time" in the family life cycle.

When an event does not take place "on time," a crisis may result. An example of this is the "empty nest" stage of the family life cycle. Many mothers face an adjustment when the last child leaves home. But this is a predictable stage which can be planned for in advance. But it is when the child *does not* leave home at the intended time that a crisis often occurs for both parent and child.[3]

My wife and I entered the empty nest approximately seven years ahead of schedule. When our daughter left home to be on her own, we should have been left with a thirteen-year-old son at home. But he had left home at the age of eleven to live at Salem Christian Home in Ontario, California. He is a profoundly mentally retarded child who is like an infant. We had planned for his leaving for two years by praying, talking, and making specific plans and steps to follow. Therefore, his leaving and our daughter's leaving were fairly easy transitions. But when our daughter told us a year and a half later that she wanted to come back home and live for a while, it was a more difficult adjustment. Why? We had adjusted to the empty nest, we liked it, and we did not expect her to come back home.

Why is the timing such an important factor? Think about it. What happens if your child does not move from junior high to high school on schedule? Or your promotional plans are delayed for two years? What happens when your twenty-year-old does not move out but decides to live at home for four more years? Or you find out you can't retire at sixty but have to work four more years while your spouse retires at sixty?

Having an event happen too early or too late in our plan can deprive us of the support of others the same or close to the same age as we are. What happens if a woman wants a child early in her married life but doesn't have one until age thirty-seven? She may not have the support of other women her own age. The mothers of children the same age as hers are much younger and they are not likely to be the ones with whom she becomes close friends.

When an event is off schedule, you may also be deprived of the sense of pride and satisfaction which often accompanies such an event. For example, some people have refined their program for promotion and advancement in their work. But what happens if that sought-after promotion occurs a year prior to retirement rather than the expected fifteen years before? Is this really recognition for accomplishment, or merely a token gesture? When an event occurs later than expected, its meaning is often lessened.

If an event occurs too early we may be limited in our preparations. A young mother widowed early has to support her family during a time when most of her friends are couples. The oldest son has to quit high school to help in the family business because of some unexpected crisis. They do not have time to prepare for their new roles. And if too many such events occur at once, we cry out, "Oh, no! Not something else!" We fold when the last straw hits us.

What can you do to prepare for and handle the predictable changes? What can you do to handle the unpredictable? The first step is to read books and resources which deal with these issues. The second step is to build a biblical perspective on life and all that it holds for us. (This last suggestion will be covered more extensively in a later chapter.)

To prepare for life's transitions, read my book, *The Seasons of a Marriage*. I would also encourage men to read *Seasons of a Man's Life* by Daniel Levinson (Random House) and *The Friendless American Male* by David Smith (Regal).

What can we learn from those who seem to cope better with the predictable changes of life as well as some of the sudden ones? These are people who face life and prepare in advance. They are also able to adjust and sort out which crisis needs to be handled first. For example, one man was facing the crisis of his wife being seriously ill in the hospital. And then the next day a major crisis threatened his business. Instead of attempting to juggle both and deal with them, he decided that his wife's recovery was most important and nothing else was going to deter him from helping her. Thus in his own mind the business crisis receded in importance. The second crisis did not add as much to his level of stress as you might expect. By making the decision he did, he was able to stay in control. That is very important. When we feel as though we are in control, we handle life better.

If you find that you are facing or in the midst of a transition, here are some suggestions.

1. Look at the stage of life you are leaving. Are you fighting leaving it in any way? What is there that you do not want to give up or change? What makes you uncomfortable with the new role? What would make you more comfortable? Find someone with whom you can discuss your answers to these questions.

2. If you are having difficulty making a decision regarding a new change or determining what plan to follow, seek the advice of someone you respect and whose insights will help you.

3. Make a specific list of what is involved in making this change in your life. Look for the information through reading and asking others about their own experiences.

4. Identify specifically what you need to do at this time which will help you feel as though you have some control of the situation. And remember that being in control does not

mean that you have all of the answers, nor do you know the outcome or when the situation will be resolved. Being in control means that you have given yourself permission not to have all of these questions answered. You have told yourself that you can handle the uncertainty. Being in control means that you have allowed Jesus Christ to come and stand with you in this time of uncertainty. His presence gives you the stability and control you need. Christ's strength is what you need. "My grace is sufficient for thee: for my strength is made perfect in weakness" (2 Corinthians 12:9 KJV).

Transitions are an opportunity to apply our faith. And we as believers have a greater opportunity to handle crisis than others. Hear what David Morley says about this.

> The change that is so threatening to the nonbeliever is an opportunity for the Christian to exercise his faith and to experience the process of true Christian maturity. The mature Christian is a person who can deal with change. He can accept all of the vicissitudes of life and not deny nor complain about them. He sees them all as the manifestation of God's love. If God loves me, then He is going to provide an experience that makes life richer and more in line with His will. To the Christian, "All things work together for good to them that love God . . ." (Romans 8:28). How often we hear that Scripture quoted. How little we see it applied to real-life experiences. What God is really saying is that we should comfort ourselves with the thought that what happens in our lives, victory or defeat, wealth or poverty, sickness or death, all are indications of God's love and His interest in the design of our lives. If He brings sickness to us, we should be joyful for the opportunity to turn to Him more completely. So often in the bloom of health, we forget to remember the God who has provided that health. When we are in a position of weakness, we are more likely to acknowledge His strength, we are more likely to ask His guidance every step of the way.[4]

4

Are You a Crisis Waiting to Happen?

▽

In my counseling practice I see many different types of people. Some of them are experiencing some type of crisis when they come in. Others are on the verge of a crisis, but they don't realize it. We in the counseling ministry can actually predict that certain individuals are crisis prone and will probably experience a self-induced crisis within the coming year. This doesn't take any great insight on my part, nor am I psychic. There are simply some people whose lifestyle and personality characteristics indicate they are on the verge of a crisis which will not only affect them but others as well.

Who are these people? Are you one of them? What are the indications? Let's consider a type which may apply to you or to a family member.

A few years ago, a raging fire swept through the hills where I was raised. This was just one of many fires that have consumed portions of Laurel Canyon, above Hollywood in Southern California. I was away on a trip and heard the news that the fire had come within fifty feet of the home in which I lived as a boy. When I returned home I drove up to Laurel Canyon and was a bit stunned to see the devastation on the ridge across from my former home. Homes which had been beautiful and alive and full were now charred and empty shells. The silence was in contrast to the sounds of life and enjoyment which had once filled the air.

Fireplaces and ashes remained and a few windowframes in some of the homes. Some homes seemed to be intact until you walked in and realized that the entire inside had been gutted by flames. The outer shell was there but the inside was burned out. This happens to people as well. They burn out. And when they do they enter into a crisis which can affect others. Burnout is on the increase and no one is immune. That's the bad news. The good news is, it doesn't have to occur.

What is *burnout?* It is a state of fatigue or frustration which has been brought about by devotion to some cause or way of life or even a relationship that failed to bring about the expected reward. In other words, the person's expectations were too high to attain and eventually the person has nothing more to give to it. Burnout also means to drain or deplete or exhaust yourself physically and mentally. It means we can wear ourselves out by excessive striving to reach some unrealistic expectation imposed on us by ourselves or someone else. Burnout is also a pattern of emotional exhaustion experienced by those in the caring professions. They give and give and give to others until their well runs dry. They feel drained and used up.

How do you know if you are leaning that way? Take this simple test and then let's consider the results.

> Look back over the past six months. Have you noticed any changes in yourself or in the world around you? Think of the office . . . the family . . . social situations. Allow about 30 seconds for each answer. Then assign it a number from 1 (for no or little change) to 5 (for a great deal of change) to designate the degree of change you perceive.
>
> 1. Do you tire more easily? Feel fatigued rather than energetic?
> 2. Are people annoying you by telling you, "You don't look so good lately"?

3. Are you working harder and harder and accomplishing less and less?

4. Are you increasingly cynical and disenchanted?

5. Are you often invaded by a sadness you can't explain?

6. Are you forgetting (appointments, deadlines, personal possessions)?

7. Are you increasingly irritable? More short-tempered? More disappointed in the people around you?

8. Are you seeing close friends and family members less frequently?

9. Are you too busy to do even routine things like make phone calls or read reports or send out your Christmas cards?

10. Are you suffering from physical complaints (aches, pains, headaches, a lingering cold)?

11. Do you feel disoriented when the activity of the day comes to a halt?

12. Is joy elusive?

13. Are you unable to laugh at a joke about yourself?

14. Does sex seem like more trouble than it's worth?

15. Do you have very little to say to people?

Very roughly, now, place yourself on the Burnout scale. Keep in mind that this is merely an approximation of where you are, useful as a guide on your way to a more satisfying life. Don't let a high total alarm you, but pay attention to it. Burnout is reversible, no matter how far along it is. The higher number signifies that the sooner you start being kinder to yourself, the better.

THE BURNOUT SCALE

0–25   You're doing fine.
26–35   There are things you should be watching.
36–50   You're a candidate.
51–65   You're burning out.
over 65 You're in a danger place, threatening to your physical and mental well-being.[1]

Burnout is a complex process which involves five major areas of life: physical, intellectual, emotional, social, and spiritual.

The *physical* refers to the amount of energy to do what you need to do and want to do. Burnout's first symptom is an all-around feeling of fatigue. Usually people suffering from burnout are not involved in exercise, or a nutrition or stress reduction program.

The *intellectual* refers to the sharpness with which a person thinks and solves problems. In burnout this ability diminishes. Creativity diminishes, cynicism increases, and there is no hobby or other means of intellectual relaxation.

The *emotional* refers to whether your emotional life is basically positive or negative. Are you optimistic or pessimistic about what is occurring in your life? Are there emotional outlets available other than work? Are you aware of what is happening to you emotionally? If you are overinvested in work and work begins to deteriorate, your personal life can begin to go downhill as well. Depression can set in because of the loss of dreams and expectations which have been so tied into work. People with a balanced life of outside interests have a buffer against burnout.

The *social* area of life refers to feelings of involvement compared to feelings of isolation. A major question is, "What kind of social support system do you have?"

Do you feel free to share your feelings of frustration, anger, fatigue, or disillusionment? Do you have anyone who will listen? Unfortunately, when a person is experiencing burnout, you often do not want to burden anyone else with your problems, thus creating further isolation for yourself.

The *spiritual* area refers to the degree of meaning a person has in his or her life. If your expectations concerning your work have been dashed, you begin to feel a void in your life. You dream about life. Your expectations about what God was supposed to do for you may be a source of disappointment.

All of the factors mentioned refer to the symptoms of burnout. Some burnout can be simply physical. A person is tired of his job, of the hours, of the ineffectiveness of the system. But he recovers after a short vacation or even just a day off. Any type of change which brings about a new interest or variation of the work routine may help.

The major symptom of burnout is the most serious and it can happen to Christians and non-Christians alike. This is long term and it is the *psychological burnout* which includes the intellectual, emotional, social, and spiritual. The symptoms of this include a decline in happiness, empathy, sensitivity, and compassion. This burnout occurs gradually and is noticeable when a crisis occurs. The relationships in all areas of life are affected. Recreation becomes mechanical, you are aloof and distant with friends, hold your emotions inside, and then are insensitive to family members.

Psychological burnout takes longer to occur and, naturally, longer from which to recover. Days off or vacations or a one-day seminar on stress or burnout are not enough. Time and a reorientation to life are what is needed. And from our perspective a spiritual renewal through the Word, prayer, and close Christian friends will also be part of the cure. Part of the reversal will also involve looking at the work environment which can contribute to the deterioration. But it really isn't circumstances. The Word of God clearly tells us that we will not be free of problems just because our circumstances are calm and peaceful. The promise of peace is a learned response which comes from application of God's Word in the midst of difficulty.

What Causes Burnout?

What causes burnout? Is it a disease with germs carried about by the winds of life? Where does it originate? There are numerous causes but two of the major ones are expectations and distribution. Unrealistic expectations about life, people, or an occupation can lead to burnout. Some individuals focus upon the goal that they wish to accomplish with no regard to the struggle involved in the attainment process.

Many individuals have been sheltered from the realities of an occupation. Thus their dreams of changing the world can be shattered easily. The pain and struggle of life has not been presented to them. When they realize they cannot change the system, idealism turns to cynicism.

Another expectation which contributes to burnout is the belief that *"it can't happen to me."* Other people collapse, but not me. Other people fail, but not me. Other people burn out, but not me.

The second major contributor to burnout is distribution. The authors of *Beyond Burnout* compare distribution to two geographic phenomena:

> . . . One is Death Valley, and the other is the Dead Sea.
> Death Valley is a desert. It is interesting because it was once an ocean teeming with life. It supported vast societies, giving life to creatures and life forms no longer present on the planet. It gave all of that for untold eons. But something changed. Oceans need feeding. Water flows from somewhere to give life to the ocean so that it might in turn give life. Whatever fed the ocean that became Death Valley stopped. Although there was nothing coming in, the ocean still tried to feed the societies that depended on it for life. It gave so much that it dried up and became not an ocean but a desert. Death Valley is a phenomenon of nature in which there is an outlet but no inlet. It simply gave up what it had and, since nothing new was coming in, it died.
>
> Think how that might describe some people. They are asked to give of themselves day in and day out. Teachers, social workers, ministers, and police officers all have demands made on them by others. If they believe that they can continually give without somehow being fed themselves, then they become psychological Death Valleys, unable to give anymore, unable to sustain life anymore. They become hollow, drained, sterile. They are the teachers without life in them. Their classrooms are infertile. They are incapable of creating a climate in which young things can grow. They are the fathers whose kisses are always dry; they are unable to give the warm, wet kisses of affection that enable their families to grow and develop. They are persons who have no sustenance coming in from outside themselves. They have dried up.
>
> The Dead Sea is a body of water that is stagnant. The Jordan River flows into the Dead Sea. It was once a body of water that supported life, but it no longer does so. It has an inlet but no outlet. It collects the waters of the Jordan River, accepts

life, and then doesn't let it out again, with the result that it is smothered and dies. Nothing escapes from the Dead Sea. It has nowhere to go. It takes everything in but lets nothing out.

There are people who, for one reason or another, are unable to let anything out. There are people who have more than they need. They have no ability to share the richness of themselves. They collect their emotions and hold them in. Never getting out, those feelings fester, become cancerous, and eat away, so that the persons again become devoid of life. They bloat with collected human expressions, experience, joys, and sadnesses. They don't know how to give. They are the physicians who are unable to reach out a hand to a dying patient. They are the athletes who forever pretend that they are on the playing field and never come to the rest of life. They are the nurses who tell little boys that cuts and broken arms don't hurt because all of their own feelings have been smothered in their own internal Dead Sea. They take everything and they give nothing back.[2]

What then can help? We need expectations and hopes in life. But if we can learn to avoid expectations which set us up for failure we will achieve a better balance. Not every student will like a teacher nor will every patient like a doctor. Many do not have the capacity to give us the recognition or appreciation that we think we need. We may not be able to radically change the problems in our profession. If we can avoid distribution systems which are draining or create isolation we will be able to maintain a better balance. Giving day after day with no outside support systems or personal enrichment and feeding soon leaves us dry. Many ministers have lost the joy of ministry because of this very problem.

But are some people more prone to burnout than others? Yes, they are and from what we can gather from available studies, here are some of characteristics of those who are more prone than others. Underachievers and happy-go-lucky individuals need not be too concerned about burnout. But dynamic, goal-oriented men and women or those who are overly idealistic and want their work, their family, their marriage, and so on to be the best, are candidates. Those who are overcommitted and overdedicated are in this category.

Generally speaking, candidates for burnout are people who are:

1. Weak and unassertive in dealing with people. They have difficulty setting limits in helping people.

2. Impatient and intolerant. They become easily frustrated.

3. Unconfident, often leading to overinvolvement and inability to say "no."

Those who are in the caring professions, and have some of the previous characteristics, are high risk candidates for burnout.

The male mid-life crisis is somewhat similar to burnout. All men do not go through this. In fact, it is only a minority who do, even though all men go through a mid-life transition. The men who are candidates for mid-life crisis are those who do not share their emotions or feelings, build their identity and sense of self-esteem through their work or vocation, and who do not have close male friendships. (For a complete discussion of the male mid-life crisis and how to resolve it, see my *Seasons of a Marriage* [Regal]).

How to Prevent Burnout

What can a person do or become to both prevent burnout and deal with it when it occurs?

There are three steps.

One, become aware of your own tendencies and determine whether you are headed in that direction or if the fire has already been ignited. Ask yourself:

1. Do I feel under pressure to succeed *all* the time?

2. Do I need to generate excitement again and again to keep from feeling bored?

3. Is one area of my life disproportionately important to me?

4. Do I feel a lack of intimacy with the people around me?

5. Am I unable to relax?

6. Am I inflexible once I've taken a stand on something?

7. Do I identify so closely with my activities that if they fall apart, I do too?

8. Am I always worried about preserving my image?

9. Do I take myself too seriously?

10. Are my goals unclear, shifting back and forth between long-range and immediate?

> Once you've thought about the questions, ask yourself if this is how you want to be. Is it how you started out being? If not, when did things change? Are you in charge of your life? Or has it taken charge of you? By fostering this kind of awareness, you will eventually get in touch with that real you that you have become so estranged from, and some of your detachment will vanish. At this point, you'll be able to start rethinking your objectives and reshaping your patterns. You will begin to differentiate between your authentic goals and the ones foisted upon you by the expectations of others.[3]

Second, incorporate the suggestions from the next chapter on the Type A person into your own life.

Third, read to become more aware of the threat of burnout. Two excellent books are *Burnout: How to Beat the High Cost of Success* by Herbert J. Freudenberger (Bantam) and *Burnout, The Cost of Caring* by Christian Maslach (Prentice-Hall).

5

The Type A Personality—
A Walking Crisis

▽

Don arrived at his office two hours early as usual. He knew he had more to do today than three people could accomplish. No one piled on this much work. He created it himself. His sense of irritation was already beginning to rise. He wished his staff would arrive early and help. Don was already beginning to walk fast. He made a long distance call and at the same time looked through a report. He glanced at the clock again and hurried even more. As he talked with an associate over the phone, he became irritated and then very angry. He shouted and then slammed down the phone. Looking at his watch again, he dialed another number, grabbed another file, stood up to see if his secretary had arrived yet, and abruptly asked for his party on the phone. Another day had started very much like every other day.

More and more we are hearing about the Type A personality who holds in his hand the potential for multiple crises. The Type A person deeply affects the lives of others, often producing family disruption, emotional and/or physical abuse, stress, a stunting of the development of family member's self-esteem, divorce, and untimely death. The Type A personality can be a man or a woman. The characteristics of this personality are very similar whether it be male or female.[1]

What is Type A behavior? It is a continuous struggle, an attempt to achieve more and more, or participate in more and more activities in less and less time. The Type A person charges ahead, often in the face of either real or imagined opposition from others. Type A personalities are dominated by an inner hidden insecurity about their status, or hyperaggressiveness, or both. Hyperaggressiveness is being overbearing and overdominating without regard for the feelings and rights of others.

The insecurity or hyperaggressiveness actually causes the struggle to start. This struggle leads then to a sense of time urgency which has been called the hurry up sickness. And as the person continues his or her inner struggle, the hyperaggressiveness and even the status insecurity manifests itself in anger. This anger is often reflected in a free-floating hostility and cynicism. If the inner struggle becomes severe and lasts over a long period of time, it leads to self-destruction.

If the Type A person, who is insecure about his status, confronts situations that are irritating, status threatening, or frustrating, he may erupt with irritation, abruptness, and internal anger. Perhaps you have experienced this or you have a family member who acts this way.

What Are Type A Persons Like?

How can you tell if you have a tendency toward Type A behavior? Let's begin by asking ourselves why the Type A person struggles so to become more involved or to accomplish so much. It is not obvious but it is very simple—there is a hidden *lack of self-esteem*. Doubts about himself are based upon what he, himself, thinks of himself. He compares himself (inaccurately) with others. His achievements cannot keep up with his unrealistic expectations. There's an inner feeling of guilt that doesn't go away.

The Type A person is also plagued with *excessive aggressiveness*. This involves not only a strong competitive desire to win, but to dominate without regard for the rights and feelings of others. The person can become upset if he doesn't win at even minor business or social activities. He views everything as a challenge.

The Type A person experiences *free-floating hostility,* a sense of lasting, indwelling anger. It increases in frequency to even minor frustrations. The Type A person is quite clever at hiding this tendency. He finds excuses and reasons for his irritation. But he becomes upset too frequently and well out of proportion. He is overly and outwardly critical and belittles and demeans others.

Because of his anger, it is difficult for the person to attract or accept affection and to give and receive love. He rarely can say that he loves another person.

The Type A person's *sense of time urgency* manifests itself in two ways. (1) He speeds up his activities. The way the person, either man or woman, thinks, plans, and carries out tasks is accelerated. He speaks faster and forces others to do the same. It is difficult to relax around him. Everything must be done faster, and the person looks for ways to increase the speed. Shaving and bathing or doing the hair must be done faster. He tries to read faster, write faster, eat faster, drive faster, and so on. Any delays or interruptions create irritation. He interrupts others to show them better and faster ways of doing things. Even though he knows better, he punches the elevator button several times to speed it up. As he arrives at a street corner, he pushes the button on the signal on each corner, and then whichever light turns green first, he goes that direction.

(2) The Type A person has many different thoughts and activities on the burner at the same time. Leisure time does not reduce the tension. He overschedules activities even during leisure time. He attempts to find more time and tries to do two or three things at once. He overextends himself in a multitude of activities and projects, and often some go undone. A juggler would be a good description of this person. When doing

projects he calls attention to himself and what he does. He will take credit for accomplishments that belongs to others.

When he eats or talks on the phone, he is also reading or shuffling through papers. He may have two TV's on while writing memos, and so on. The list goes on and the person is proud of his juggling act! What about you? Does this description fit you in any way? Does it describe a family member?

The last characteristic of many Type A's is an unconscious drive to _self-destruction._ They make major mistakes and some even mention that they will succumb to the stress they are bringing upon themselves. The _Type A person is five times more likely to have a heart attack_ than the Type B person which we will discuss in a moment.[2] Think of that as a potential crisis.

What are the actual results of Type A behavior? According to Friedman and Ulmer, a Type A person is responsible for "repeated disasters—careers and lives wrecked, whole businesses and large enterprises threatened with ruin."[3] This type of behavior also causes devastating effects on marital relations and parent-child relationships. All of these become full-blown crises. One of the additional concerns is the physical damage which occurs. There are three arterial diseases which it is believed that Type A behavior either initiates or worsens: migraines, high blood pressure, and coronary heart disease.[4]

Little has been said about the Type B personality. But it is important to understand this personality as well since the Type A person lacks some very valuable qualities the Type B possesses. Type B's do not lead dull and boring lives. They are creative, productive, and enjoy life. They do not have the sense of time urgency. They are able to accomplish without the frenzy and rage of the Type A person. They possess patience and feel secure enough not to have to rush to finish every task on a deadline basis. They delegate authority with the expectation that others will do it differently and within a different time frame. They reflect on life and also on what they like about themselves. They have learned to value and enjoy life and themselves as much or more for what has already been accomplished or experienced than for what may occur in the future. They don't create crises for themselves and others.

All Type B personalities have one important characteristic in common: they do not have free-floating hostility. They can handle stress and have the capacity for empathy—putting themselves in another person's shoes. They have a positive sense of self-esteem which is not based upon their accomplishments. They also have an intact personality.

Can a Type A Person Change?

If you are a Type A, what can you do? Are you doomed to be this way forever? Is it really possible to change from being a Type A to a Type B? The answer is definitely yes.

The first step is to admit that you suffer from the disease of time urgency. Too many people have come to regard it as a normal way of living.

Why are you (or a family member) this way? In most cases it stems from insecurities and low self-esteem. The main fear is that sooner or later you will be unable to cope with some task or situation. Because of that you feel you will lose status and prestige in the eyes of your superiors and peers. You fear you do not have the ability to perform.

Now is the time to identify and replace your beliefs with new ones. Here are some typical erroneous beliefs shared by Type A persons:

"My sense of time urgency helps me gain social and economic success." You actually struggle for success but it doesn't come as you want it to. Any *success* which you have attained has come from something *other* than the time urgency. Review the *failures* of your life and you will discover that most of them have come from this sense of time urgency.

"I can't do anything about my life" and "My insecurity is too deep-seated to change." Both of these beliefs are false. If you desire to change, invite Jesus Christ to be the change agent in your life. (Please read chapter 3 of my *Making Peace* with Your Past for expanded information on letting Jesus Christ change your life.)

A major step toward improvement is to take the time to build an adequate sense of self-esteem, for the Type A person has a damaged personality.

To help repair your personality or a family member's, read chapter 2 of Making Peace with Your Past, then listen to the tapes by Dr. David Seamands, Damaged Emotions, The Healing of the Memories, My Grace Is Sufficient for You, The Spirit of a Person, The Hidden Tormentors, Is Your God Fit to Love?, and The Hidden Child in Us All. Sit in a quiet room and listen to the tapes without doing any other task. Don't listen while driving. Then read Do I Have to Be Me? by Dr. Lloyd Ahlem (Regal) or my Improving Your Self-Image.

Changing your life or helping a family member change involves learning to express yourself in new ways, using emotional words, or by using similes or metaphors. This can be done by reading books or poetry, observing the style of the writer, and then beginning to use more descriptive words.

As one Type A put it, "I don't have time for thinking about my past, for developing friendships with others and family members. That's a waste of time. So what if I talk like a computer? I don't use descriptive adjectives because it takes too much time to use adjectives and figures of speech. That's ridiculous. I just have to strive for more and more things in my life." Unfortunately, however, this striving is done at the expense of the things worth doing.

Cultivate new relationships. This could involve calling or writing old friends and relatives, or taking your spouse out on a dinner date every week or two weeks. Leave your wrist watch at home and don't talk about work or accomplishments.

Steps toward Wholeness

Choose four or five of the following activities to begin practicing each week until both you and others around you are able to see a change. This may be uncomfortable at first since you are giving up a way of life that is both comfortable and potentially destructive. But it is worth the effort.

1. Each day think about the cause for your time urgency. Write down one of the consequences.

2. As part of your new program read *When I Relax I Feel Guilty* by Tim Hansel (David C. Cook) in a leisurely fashion.

3. Reduce your tendency to think and talk rapidly by making a conscious effort to listen to others. Become "A Ready Listener" (James 1:19 AMP). Ask questions to encourage others to continue talking. If you have something to say, ask yourself: Who really wants to hear this? Is this the best time to share it?

4. Begin each day by asking God to help you prioritize those items that need to be done first. Then do only those items which you really have time for. If you feel you can accomplish five during the day, do only four.

5. If you begin to feel pressured about completing your tasks, ask yourself these questions: Will completing this task matter three to five years from now? Must it be done now? If so, why? Could someone else do it? If not, why?

6. Try to accomplish only one thing at a time. If you are going to the bathroom, don't brush your teeth at the same time. If you are waiting for someone on the phone, don't attempt to look through the mail or a magazine. Instead, gaze at a restful picture, or do some relaxation exercises. When someone is talking to you, put down your newspaper, magazine, or work and give the person your full attention.

7. Try to relax without feeling guilty. Give yourself permission to relax and enjoy yourself. Tell yourself it is all right because indeed it is. Relaxation is a key ingredient in good health.

8. Reevaluate your need for recognition. Instead of looking for the approval of others, tell yourself in a realistic way, "I did a good job and I can feel all right about it."

9. Begin to look at the Type A behavior of others. Ask yourself, "Do I really like that person's behavior and the way

he or she responds to people? Do I want to be that way?"

10. Since you have a tendency to think in numbers such as "How much?" and "How many?" change the way you evaluate others or situations. Express your feelings in adjectives and not numbers.

11. Begin to read magazines and books which have nothing to do with your vocation. Go to the library and check out novels or books on different topics. Become adventuresome but don't see how many different books you can read—or brag to others about this "accomplishment."

12. Play some soft background music at home or at the office to give a soothing atmosphere.

13. Attempt to plan your schedule so that you drive or commute when traffic is light. Try to drive in the slow lane of the highway or freeway. Try to reduce your tendency to drive faster than others or just as fast.

14. Don't evaluate your life in terms of how much you have accomplished or how many material things you have acquired. Recall your past enjoyable experiences for a few minutes each day. Take time to daydream about pleasurable experiences as a child.

15. Make your noon hour a rest time away from work. Go shopping, browse through stores, read, or have lunch with a friend. After a meal with a friend make notes of that person's concerns which he or she shared with you. Use this as a prayer guide. Follow up later to see how the person is doing. You may want to call a different person each week. Let them know you have been praying for them and want to know how they are doing.

16. Begin your day fifteen minutes early and do something you enjoy. If you tend to skip breakfast or eat standing up, sit down and take your time eating. Look around the house or outside and fix your interest upon something pleasant you have been overlooking such as flowers in bloom or a beautiful painting.

17. Begin to recognize what your values are. Where did they come from and how do they fit into the teaching of scrip-

ture? Spend time in the scriptures considering what God's plan is for your life. Read Lloyd Ogilvie's book, *God's Will in Your Life* (Harvest House).

18. Each day try to spend a bit of time alone. Whatever you do at this time do it slowly in a relaxed manner.

19. Begin to develop some interests and hobbies which are totally different from what you do for a living.

20. Decorate your office or work area with something new each month. Bring in flowers, a plant, a new picture, and take pride in what you do to express yourself. ˙

21. As you play games or engage in sports, whether it be racquetball, skiing, or cards, do it for the enjoyment of it and do not make it competition. Begin to look for the enjoyment of a good run, an outstanding rally, and the good feelings that come with recreation which you have been overlooking.

22. If you have a tendency to worry, begin to follow the suggestions given in my book, *The Healing of Fear* (Harvest House).

23. Allow yourself more time than you need for your work. Schedule ahead of time and for longer intervals. If you usually take a half hour for a task, allow forty-five minutes. You will see an increase in the quality of your work.

24. Evaluate what you do and why you do it. Dr. Lloyd Ogilvie offers some insights on our motivation and the pressures we create.

> We say, "Look, God, how busy I am!" We equate exhaustion with an effective, full life. Having uncertain purposes, we redouble our efforts in an identity crisis of meaning. We stack up performance statistics in the hope that we are counting for something in our generation. But for what or for whom?
>
> Many of us become frustrated and beg for time to just be, but do our decisions about our involvements affirm that plea? A Christian is free to stop running away from life in overinvolvement.[5]

In one of Dr. Ogilvie's sermons he also raised two interesting questions which relate to what we are doing and how we are doing it. "What are you doing with your life that you couldn't do without the *power of God?*" and "Are you living life out of your own *adequacy* or out of the abundance of the riches of Christ?" Both questions are something to think about.

Evaluate all that you do by making a list of all of the various activities in which you are involved. Then place each item in the proper column on this chart.

Very Crucial	Very Important	Important	Good

Everything that falls in "Very Crucial" stays in your life. Whatever falls in "Very Important" would probably stay but if necessary could be dropped. Anything that falls in "Important" can either stay or go. And anything listed under "Good" can be dropped from your life. This may be difficult and you may find it agonizing to drop just one activity. But in time you will feel a sense of relief as you consider why you do what you do and what it is doing to you.[6]

25. Each morning and each evening for a month, in a slow, calm, steady voice read aloud the following poems. Consider the wisdom of these words.

SLOW ME DOWN, LORD

Slow me down, Lord.
Ease the pounding of my heart by the quieting of my mind.
Steady my hurried pace with a vision of the eternal reach of time.
Give me, amid the confusion of the day, the calmness of the everlasting hills.
Break the tensions of my nerves and muscles with the soothing music of the singing streams that live in my memory.
Teach me the art of taking minute vacations—of slowing down to look at a flower, to chat with a friend, to pat a dog, to smile at a child, to read a few lines from a good book.
Slow me down, Lord, and inspire me to send my roots deep into the soil of life's enduring values, that I may grow toward my greater destiny.
Remind me each day that the race is not always to the swift; that there is more to life than increasing its speed.
Let me look forward to the towering oak and know that it grew great and strong because it grew slowly and well.[7]

~~~~~~~~~

I wasted an hour one morning beside a mountain stream,
I seized a cloud from the sky above and fashioned myself a dream,
In the hush of the early twilight, far from the haunts of men,
I wasted a summer evening, and fashioned my dream again.
Wasted: Perhaps. Folks say so who never have walked with God.
When lanes are purple with lilacs or yellow with goldenrod.
But I have found strength for my labors in that one short evening hour.
I have found joy and contentment; I have found peace and power.
My dreaming has left me a treasure, a hope that is strong and true.

From wasted hours I have built my life and found my faith anew.[8]

These are just some of the suggestions which can help you. Most of these suggestions have to do with your sense of time urgency and panic approach to life.[9]

Dealing with Your Anger

The next issue to consider is your free-floating hostility or anger. This hostility along with the sense of time urgency are the two main overt characteristics of Type A behavior. How can you get rid of this destructive anger?

The first step is to recognize the fact that this is a part of your life. Ask yourself the following questions and answer them honestly:

1. Do I become irritated or angry at minor mistakes of friends, family members, and acquaintances—or find mistakes hard to overlook?

2. Do I find myself critically examining a situation for the purpose of finding something that is wrong or might go wrong?

3. Do I find myself scowling and unwilling or unable to laugh at things others laugh at?

4. Am I overly proud of my ideals and enjoy telling others about them?

5. Do I believe and/or say that most people cannot be trusted? Do I believe that everyone else has a selfish motive?

6. Do I regard others with contempt?

7. Do I tend to shift the conversation to the faults or errors of others?

8. Do I regularly swear out loud or in my thoughts?

9. Do I find it difficult to compliment or congratulate others with genuine feelings?[10]

If any of these questions apply, you probably have some level of free-floating hostility.

Evaluate your level of self-esteem since it is a root cause for anger (see books mentioned earlier).

The next step is to identify and challenge the beliefs you have about your hostility. Do you believe it's necessary? Do you believe that it cannot be changed? Do you believe that other people deserve it? Once again here is a list which you can use to help the change process.

1. One of the best ways to overcome a negative habit is to make an announcement to significant people in your life of your intentions. Therefore, select those most affected by your hostility and let them know your intentions. Give these people permission to remind you of your commitment if they see your hostility on the rise. If you feel it beginning to rise, warn them verbally or with some prearranged sign. One man made a miniature flagpole to place on his desk at the office. When he was calm, the flag was green, when he started to become irritated he changed the flag to yellow and when he was angry, he promptly hoisted a red flag of warning.

2. Go out of your way to recognize the efforts and positive contributions of others and express your appreciation. You may end up with a better feeling and the others may also respond better as well.

3. In competitive games and fun games, play to lose some of the time. A side benefit of this will be that as you lessen your concentration on winning, you will improve your skills.

4. At first, avoid others who are quick to anger or other Type A's since it will take you some time to learn not to react to them.

5. Make a list of the reasons and benefits for eliminating this hostility from your life. The list may impress you with the importance of the new approach you are taking.

6. Try to identify your trigger point of anger. What irritates you the most? Why? What would happen if you did not become angry?

7. Keep a behavioral diary. Whenever anger occurs record the following:

> The circumstances surrounding the anger such as who was there, where it occurred, what triggered it, and so on.

> The specific ways you acted and the statements you made.
> The other person's reactions to your behaviors and statements.
> The manner in which the issue was eventually resolved.
> Describe what you will do next time.

It is important to develop a plan of action for interrupting your anger. This plan should involve immediate action to disengage from the situation. It should also be a way to face and handle the problem at a later time. Interrupting the conflict is an application of Nehemiah 5:6–7, "I [Nehemiah] was very angry when I had heard their outcry and these words. I counseled with myself, and contended with the nobles and the rulers" (AMP). Another version states, "I thought it over."

In your diary use this chart to keep track of your anger.

Date	Time	Intensity of Anger 1 2 3 4 5 Light Moderate High	What I Became Angry At	How I Responded

8. Read Ephesians 4:26; Proverbs 15:1, 18; 16:32; 19:11; 29:11. Write out how you see yourself applying each one of these passages to your life. Describe how you will reflect each one in your daily life.

One of the most basic and helpful ways to bring about lasting change is to look at your perception of God and come to an understanding of God's qualities and characteristics. Often we create God in our image of what He should be and fail to recognize who He really is.

What we think about God is one of the most important things about us. We tend to move toward our mental image of God. A proper perception of God is essential to one's Christian life and feelings about himself. A misperception limits our capacity for fully developing our lives. God is not a policeman, an unfair judge, or a spiteful tyrant—God is fair, just, loving, holy, righteous, faithful, and good. He does *not* say, "You must work yourself into a frazzle in order to please me and be accepted by me." The Type A person, or anyone else with low self-esteem for that matter, struggles with the feeling of inadequacy. They feel deficient and in their own way seek to fill the void. And when it doesn't occur, despondency or anger results.

Our God is a God who gives us status, forgiveness, and adequacy. None of these can be earned. Any shortage of payment was paid by Christ on the cross. Our adequacy is a gift with no strings attached. You and I have been declared to be adequate! God is saying accept it, experience it, live it, enjoy it!

(For additional treatment of self-image, see my *Improving Your Self-Image* [Harvest House] and *The Sensation of Being Somebody* by Maurice Wagner [Zondervan].)

6

Crisis in the Life of a Child

▽

Donny sat quietly in the chair. Every now and then he would look up and say, "Nothing's wrong. I don't want to be here. I want to go home and play. I feel all right." Donny appeared to be a normal eight-year-old boy but his parents were concerned. He was becoming withdrawn and quiet. On occasion his behavior was more typical of a five-year-old. His mother said, "I can't understand what's gotten into that boy. He's never acted this way before. I don't understand it. I've talked to him, scolded him, and taken him to our doctor. Nothing physical is wrong and I can't seem to shake him out of this. What's wrong?"

What was wrong with Donny? Why did he behave this way? From an adult perspective, nothing crucial had occurred. Except at school, his favorite teacher had left and a harsh new substitute had taken over. His two closest friends had moved away and he had overheard his parents talking about a divorce. Donny was in a crisis!

Do you remember what it was like to be a child? Can you take yourself back to that time and remember what life was like? Every day could hold a crisis experience for you at that age. And not only that, your skills at that age for handling a crisis were not as developed or extensive as they are now.

A child going to a new school or new church or even a summer camp could perceive each experience as a scary threat. A low grade on a test, a pet running away, or the rejection of a friend could produce an upset equal in intensity to the emotional upheaval of a crisis. If you are a parent or a person who works with children, it is important to be able to identify the signs of a crisis in a child and give him or her the assistance needed at that time. Your sensitivity as an adult will develop by listening to your child both with your eyes and with your ears.

Crisis in a child of any age can have long-lasting effects since it may make the child less capable of dealing with trauma in the future. This is an actual fact based upon substantial research. It is one of the reasons why parents need to adequately prepare themselves and their children for life's difficulties. It is interesting to note that many parents talk with their child about sex, right and wrong, how to be polite, how to get along with their friends. But how many parents talk with children about how to handle disappointments and upsets? It is definitely a neglected area which has repercussions.

A child copes with a crisis in a different manner than an adult. Why? Because the child is more limited in his or her coping skills.

For a child, there are two main stages involved in resolving a crisis. The first stage involves the initial shock which leads to a high level of anxiety. This is difficult for the child to handle as compared to an adult, since adults have more previous experiences to draw upon. Children do not have as many experiences to use as a stabilizing factor. They don't always know that the problem will be resolved. They may feel as though they are in the midst of a never-ending tornado. A child's mind and emotional state is not yet developed enough to solve problems as an adult. We as adults can rely upon resources and established routines but children tend to fall back on the chaos of the situation. An adult can use questions such as, "Why did this have to happen to me?" or "Why do I have to go through all this and suffer?" to help him wrestle with a problem. But a child's mind is not developed to this extent and cannot deal with such philosophical thoughts. In a way children lose their identity or sense of self in a crisis.

The second state of the crisis is similar but less intense. This is the time when the child is able to look at the crisis and evaluate it instead of just responding to it. It is still hard for the child to adjust at this stage. Adults relive the crisis again and again in their minds. They daydream about their past life and by doing this create some future hopes for a new beginning. All of this is what we call the work of grieving. And eventually we feel stronger and once again in control. We have the capability of picking up our lives and going on.

This is where a child experiences some difficulty. A child lacks the verbal skills and the creative fantasy ability which we as adults have developed. This is a deficit for a child. Because of having a more limited repertoire of solutions, children tend to cling to inadequate ones to solve their problems. Adults often go to friends for advice, support, and comfort. This helps to bring about a clearer perspective. But children don't always realize that they have the same opportunities. For a child, talking increases his anxiety and thus he tends not to talk.

If a child continues to be anxious and not live up to his or her potential, he will remain in this second stage. This means that the attempts to adequately resolve the crisis have failed. And some of the energy that should be used to deal with life and future crisis is diverted to dealing with this unresolved issue. This then makes a child more vulnerable to stress. And then the child feels bad about his or her inability to cope. Unresolved crises weaken us as we go through life. And if a child experiences a series of crises which remain unresolved, this pattern of repeated losses leads them to helplessness.

Some adults are capable of handling crisis by restricting their lives and their activities in some manner. This is one way to regain stability and control. But children too often do not have this option. They have to continually face their daily challenges. They can't skip school or some of their other involvements. Sometimes we ask too much of children.

A child needs to discuss and sort out his fears with an adult since he probably does not realize that he has other options.

One of the most characteristic responses of a child involved in a crisis is regression. When a child responds at his appropriate age level, he is then capable of knowing how to use his skills and capabilities properly to relate to others and confront tasks and problems. But during a time of upset, such as in a crisis, he loses his capacity to bring together all of his knowledge and capabilities to meet this problem situation. He becomes confused and disorganized. And he then responds as he did when he was younger.[1]

If you want to help your child, be empathetic. Empathy means entering the private world of your child and becoming comfortable with it. It's realizing that your child's thinking and perception are different from yours as an adult.

Empathy means moving into the child's world for a time *without* making judgments or giving advice.

Empathy means sensing meanings of events of which the child is not aware. It means putting your thoughts and help into words the child can understand.

Your main purpose in empathy is clarifying your child's jumbled feelings. He may experience a number of confusing feelings all at the same time. Unraveling these will help him solve problems according to his ability.[2]

Communication is a key in helping children in crisis. You may feel you can communicate with children, but do the children feel that you are communicating with them? Children have their own style of reasoning, meanings for words, and connections for events. You must enter their frame of reference if you are going to be able to minister to them. A child's thought pattern will follow its own logic and not yours. And what makes sense to you may make no sense to the child.

It is important to look at children's thinking and communication at different stages in order to minister to them in crisis. Let's look at the difference at the various age levels.[3]

The Magic Years

The *magic years* (ages three to six) are the years of early childhood, nursery school, and kindergarten. And children this age do experience crisis. We call this the time of magical thinking because the child's belief at this stage includes believing that his own thought processes can influence objects and events in the world outside himself. He is unable to understand how and why things happen, how and why life is unpredictable. Adults accept sudden events as just a part of life. Scripture teaches us that life is uncertain and we should expect problems and upsets to occur. But children have a difficult time grasping this.

A child at this age does not understand that his thoughts do not cause an event to occur. A child's thinking reflects omnipotence. He believes he is at the center of life and can affect what happens. Children do not understand why they become ill. They become quite disturbed with the unfamiliar bodily changes that accompany illness. And they often believe that they caused the illness. A cold is a punishment because they were bad.

If this is how they think, what can you do as a parent? Sometimes it will be impossible to fully change the child's pattern of thinking. Accept this as a fact of life and this will help lessen your own frustration. Helping your child fully express his inner thoughts and feelings is one of your best approaches. This helps him gain greater self-control in a crisis event. By expressing his thoughts aloud, he can move to a new position. Patiently repeat your questions to the child, and encourage him to think aloud. Let him know that it's all right to talk like this. Help him discover the most probable or real reason for what occurred. And try to help him discover this himself instead of giving him the reason. This takes time and your frustration may cause you to become impatient and tell the child what is happening. Look for any indications of guilt that the child may be experiencing.

Young children are egocentric; they are self-centered. They feel the world revolves around them. They fail to consider the viewpoints of others. This has nothing to do with being conceited, it is just a normal part of the developmental process. Children of this age talk past one another. They have their own private speech and may not be talking to anyone in particular. They are not concerned whether the listener understands their words or not. They just assume their words have more meaning than is there. They take things for granted and do not realize that other people need clarification. When a child reaches the age of seven, he begins to learn to distinguish between his perspective and someone else's.

As a parent, you need to use the child's language and be flexible in your communication. You must actively guide your conversation with a young child or you will end up with a failure to communicate.

A young child takes things at face value, very literally. If you say, "I'm sick and tired of the way you are acting," what does a child think? He catches your anger but also believes that you may be getting both "sick" and "tired." Think of the other phrases we say that are misunderstood. "Keep your shirt on," "hold your horses," "that's cool," and so on. Try to enter the child's mind. If you could hear what he is thinking, you would be amazed!

A child puts two and two together and does not necessarily come up with four as the answer. His connections are unique. Those connections make sense to him but to no one else. A child may see illness and going to the football game as related because his father became seriously ill the last time he went to the football game. A child may even become very anxious and avoid going to a game because of the connection he made between the game and his father's illness.

Young children often center on one aspect of an event to the exclusion of all the others. They cannot see the forest for the trees. If you give too much information and too many events to a child in your conversations, he cannot handle them. Introduce other aspects of the situation to a child gradually as he is ready to handle them. Help the child see all the aspects, to organize his thoughts, to explore other reasons for what happened. One of the best descriptions I have heard is that helping children is like working on a jigsaw puzzle. You help them by asking them to discover the other pieces, by pointing out some of the pieces, and by helping fit these pieces together.

Remember these facts as you try to help your child: the child feels responsible for what happened; he makes different connections from yours; he is egocentric; and he centers on one event to the exclusion of others. He needs you to be a good listener.

The Middle Years

Children from seven to twelve have changed considerably in their thinking. They have advanced in their ability to think conceptually. They are now able to work out problems in their heads instead of just by trial and error. They can see the viewpoints of other people, and they recognize the feelings of others as well. Even their fantasy world has changed. They now fantasize about real people and events instead of so much make believe.

Children in the middle years are usually enjoyable and uncomplicated, calm and educable. But they still have a difficult time dealing with anything that resembles a crisis situation. They prefer to avoid the issue and often will change the subject when you attempt to draw them into a discussion of their problem. They try to avoid the pain and anxiety. This is why many who work with children of this age use games and play in the therapy process. Play allows children an outlet for what they are feeling and gives the therapist the information sought after. Communication toys such as tape recorders, phones, drawing materials, and puppets are very helpful even for parents to use.

Even though these children have developed considerably in their thinking processes they still tend to jump to conclusions without considering all the facts. In fact, children of this age group have a tendency to listen to contradictory information and not see the inconsistency. They often do not understand what they are hearing. Sometimes these children will not understand adults who are talking to them, and the problem is that the adults do not realize they are not being understood. As you work with a child, you need to make your statements very clear and even rephrase the statement several times. Repeat and repeat. What may be clear to you may not register with the child.

Based upon the way children think, listen, and reason, what additional approaches can you take when you try to help your child in a crisis situation? Be flexible, and be able to shift gears as you work with your child.

Be sure you do not attempt to force your adult logic upon your child. Listen to the way your child communicates for that is a key to knowing how to communicate back. Children are walking question marks. They ask questions for information and as their roundabout way of letting you know something is bothering them.

Do not ask questions that can be answered with a "yes" or "no." They will be of little value to you. General questions may not bring a direct answer. Asking for comparisons can be helpful, however, such as asking your child to describe two different events or two different people.

If you don't understand what your child is saying or he or she means, don't be afraid to let him or her know. You might say, "Sally, I think I understand what you are wanting to tell me, but I am not sure. Could you tell me that again with some different words?" Reflect on how your child looks as she is talking. This lets her know you are receiving part of the message.

Children in crisis handle their problem by increasing their defenses. This is what works for them. Here is a listing of some of the defense mechanisms so you will have a better understanding of what your child and you use.

> Fantasy—daydreaming about solutions to a problem.
> Hypochondriasis—using illness as an excuse not to deal with a problem.

> Projection—blaming other people and things for their problems.
> Displacement—taking out their feelings on someone or something other than the original source.
> Repression—unconsciously blocking out strong feelings.
> Suppression—consciously holding back feelings.
> Sublimation—substituting one set of feelings for another set of more socially acceptable feelings.

How do you support a child's use of defenses? Simply go along with what your child is doing at the time as long as it is not hurting someone. A child may need to use fantasy, rationalization, or displacement for a time.

Depression in Children

Depression is no respector of persons. And it often goes undetected in our children by us as parents. Children may be the most hidden age group of all in terms of incidence of depression. We as parents often deny that our child is unhappy. We fail to recognize, accept, and respond appropriately to our child's depression. After all, who wants to admit his child is depressed? Do you know when your child is depressed? Do you know the signs and indications? Here is a composite picture of how any child would appear *if every characteristic* of depression were included.

First of all, a child may *appear* sad, depressed, or unhappy. He does not verbally complain of this, and he might not even be aware of it. But he behaves in such a way to give that impression.

Another characteristic is withdrawal and inhibition. Interest in activities is very limited. The child appears listless and parents often think he is bored or sick. Frequently a parent begins to look for some symptom of a hidden physical illness. There may be some physical symptoms which further blur the fact of depression. These symptoms include headaches, stomach aches, and sleeping or eating disturbances.

Discontent is a common mood. A child gives the impression of being dissatisfied. He or she gets little pleasure from what he does. Often people wonder, "Why is that child so unhappy? Is someone doing something to that child?" They wonder if someone else is responsible for the way the child feels.

The child may feel rejected or unloved. He may tend to withdraw from anything that may be a disappointment to him. As with other age groups, he may have a negative self-concept and even feel worthless.

Irritability and low frustration tolerance may be seen. Often the child is unaware of why he is bothered.

There are some children who, when depressed, act just the opposite. Clowning around and provoking others are their attempts to deal with their depressive feelings. They may act this way at a time of achievement because they find it difficult to handle something positive. This provocative behavior usually makes other people angry.

Children do not always experience and express their depression in the same way as adults. Because of their limited experience and physiology, they may tend to express their depression as rebellion, negativity, anger, or resentment. The depression expressed when parents divorce, for example, may be manifested by bed-wetting, attacking friends or siblings, clinging to parents, failure in school, and exaggerated storytelling.

The signs and symptoms of depression vary with the child's age. An infant who is depressed may simply not thrive. A parent's depression may also affect a small child. For example, a mother who is depressed may withdraw from her child, who in turn becomes depressed. But the child may not be able to overcome the depression until the mother overcomes her depression.

Why do children become depressed? It could be caused by any of the following: a physical defect or illness; malfunction of the endocrine glands; lack of affection, which can create insecurity in the child; lack of positive feedback and encouragement for accomplishments; death of a parent; divorce, separation, or desertion by a parent; parental favor toward one sibling;

poor relationship between a step-parent and step-child; economic problems in the home; moving to a new home or school; punishment by others.[4]

There are many depressive experiences that you can handle without taking your child for counseling. But if the depression is severe and your child does not respond, don't hesitate to seek professional help.

Your child needs to be helped to experience the depression as fully as possible. Resisting the depression does not help. It merely prolongs the experience. Encourage your son or daughter to be as honest as possible in admitting that he is depressed or sad. If grief is involved, you need to allow the child to do the grieving naturally. If the grief is over divorce, do not expect the child to get over the grief quickly. This type can last longer and can recur from time to time.

Help your child find some type of activity that will bolster him. A new game, a hobby, a sight-seeing trip, or anything that would interest him may be helpful.

Find a way for the child to experience some type of success. His self-esteem can be elevated and rediscovered by small successes.

Help the child break out of his routine. Even simple things like new food at a meal or taking him to a special restaurant may help. Taking a day off from school for an outing may be helpful unless he enjoys school more than the outing.

Listen to your child without being judgmental or critical. He needs your support.[5] If children are going to be able to handle their adult crises successfully, they need to learn how to handle the crises of childhood and adolescence as well.

7

A Time of Crisis— Adolescence

▽

Yesterday Susan, a poised, self-confident young lady of fourteen (going on twenty) left for school with all of her schoolwork finished, her bed made, and her clothes neatly put away in the closet. She came home from school, however, fourteen (going on five)—mad at her girlfriend because she wouldn't walk home with her, angry and pouting when her mother asked her to set the table for dinner. Susan's days are like that. One moment she is a mature young lady, the next moment a child. Susan is a teenager.

Remember the roller coaster? That fast, open, frightening cart on a track with sharp climbs and steeper plunges and neck-jerking sudden turns? This is also a description of adolescence. It is a roller coaster experience, a time of stress and storm as well as growth.

For some young people, adolescence is a time of continual crisis with few respites. For others, development is a bit smoother. But overall, adolescence is one of the most difficult transitions of life. It can be the time when self-doubt and feelings of inferiority are intensified and when social pressures are at their peak. An adolescent's self-worth is dependent upon one of the most unstable pillars in existence, peer acceptance. And the junior high years are probably the most critical to the development of a child's mental health.

If you are the parent of a thirteen- to nineteen-year-old, your teenager is becoming independent from you and at the same time experiencing a radical identity crisis. Many are able to establish their identity at this time, while others postpone it until adulthood.[1]

Adolescents today face a unique set of pressures. They experience instant information and a media bombardment that usually transmits values contrary to the Christian faith and beliefs. Children and youth are being raised today in a promiscuous, violent, non-Christian society. And being a Christian can create additional stress that produces inner conflict.

When did *you* make your major moral choices? Do you remember your age? Moral choices are being made at a much younger age today. These decisions include sex, drugs, friends, and drinking. Latest research indicates that one out of five junior high students has already had sexual intercourse.

Close your eyes and think with me for a moment. Try to imagine your feelings if time and time again from both the media and well-known church leaders you were told that the world is coming to an end within the next fifteen to twenty years. Think of your dreams and desires and all those experiences you are looking forward to which you will *not* experience if the world does come to an end. What goes through your mind? What do you feel?

This present generation lives under the potential of being the last generation. These kids face the possibility of having no future. Wars have always been a part of life, but never before have we had a generation that lives under the threat of being destroyed instantaneously. What do they hear from the media? The threat of war, the bomb, pollution, social security funds being exhausted, and other frightening prospects. Many young people seek to avoid these possibilities by finding pleasure wherever they can. *Their avoidance of future crisis can create a present crisis.*

More and more teens are coming from unstable homes.

Divorce is commonplace, and the role models of stable marriages and stable family life are disappearing.

This generation also tends to be unable to understand and follow through with commitment. Perhaps that is partly because they have been given much more than previous generations. Today's teens have not had to struggle as much as those growing up in the '30s, '40s, '50s, and '60s. It is difficult for them to delay rewards. They don't know how to handle discouragement and disillusionment very well. Therefore, they are prone to experience crisis more readily. They look for instant solutions. Many of them use drugs as their escape, and in some cases when nothing else will work, they opt for suicide.[2]

This is a discouraging picture, but, unfortunately, many teenagers fit into this scenario. There are many others who are committed, well-adjusted future adults, but they, too, will experience crisis situations.

Adolescence—a Transition Period

The time of adolescence is a transition period between childhood and adulthood. There are three important psychological tasks that teenagers need to accomplish. Dr. Keith Olson describes them in this manner:

1. To develop a sense of personal identity. This means a young person is trying to establish who he or she is as an integrated individual throughout each life role, separate and different from every other person. Young people struggle with wanting to be unique and yet also fit in with their friends.

2. To begin the process of establishing relationships that are characterized by commitment and intimacy.

3. To begin making decisions leading toward training and entry into a particular occupation.[3]

What happens as an adult is really based upon the successful completion of these tasks. Part of the crisis of adolescence will be tied into these developmental issues.

To be successful in future years, the adolescent needs to move away from his childhood dependence upon his parents.

But this move toward independence often creates a crisis for his parents because the parents are not in control of how this movement occurs. If the parents resist the breaking away, stress occurs for both parties. If you are the parent of a teen, how do you feel about the changes you see taking place in your young person? Let's look at some of the normal breaking-away behaviors.

The Process of Breaking Away

An adolescent needs quantity time alone and with his own age group. Jim, a quiet fifteen-year-old, never seemed to spend time with his parents. When he was at home, he seemed to hibernate in his room. But most of the time, he was off with his friends. His parents were concerned and upset because six months prior, he seemed very close to the other family members. Now they seemed to be ignored! He is not that eager for family get-togethers nor as interested in them as he used to be.

Don't be surprised if he withdraws from involvements, including church attendance. He tends to be secretive around you and does not confide in you as before. A parent who uses his child for his own identity needs and self-esteem has difficulty handling this lack of confiding and wishes for a return to the "good old days."

Teenagers are reluctant to accept advice or criticism from their parents. Tim and Sue can vouch for that. Every time they try to talk to their son about the way he dresses he stalks out of the room in anger. Teenagers are overly sensitive to suggestions because their insecurities seem to arise when they are given advice or criticism. Their lack of properly formed identity and low self-esteem tend to make them more sensitive. They resent criticism. Discipline, criticism, and advice are interpreted as domination, and they feel out of control. They need to be *in* control. But parents, too, need to feel in control. The result is conflict.

Rebellion is a common reaction. But the more secure the

teenager, the less rebellion will be seen. The more insecure, the more radical the rebellion.[4]

During the late teenage years, allegiance and commitment are shifted more to the individual peers of both the opposite and same sex. But are you aware of just how strong this shift is? The importance of this transition in a teenager's life is illustrated in the following chart.[5]

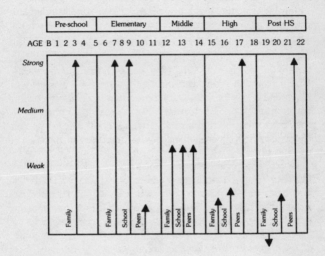

Adolescents are very dependent upon feedback from their peers.

Their children's increased involvement with their age group often creates anxiety for parents. Evenings spent talking on the telephone and constant strong demands to be with friends are perfectly normal. Changes in manners of dress, speech, musical taste, enjoyable activities, and general behavior are usually related to their friends.

Don't be surprised if adolescents are absorbed with their own world. *Self-centeredness is very common.* If adolescents are critical, they tend to assume others are also critical of them. They think of themselves as unique and special. They are satisfied with old friendships. Moving to a new location at this time of life can be traumatic.

High on their list of concerns are social fears. They don't like feeling rejected, disapproved of, or ignored. And they don't want to look foolish or be out of control! Authority figures are among those to be feared. That could include parents!

Harold was sitting in the living room. He was really indignant and upset about a situation at school. He said, "The school policy is ridiculous. It shouldn't be that way. It's not right! See if I support that school any more." His parents were taken aback because two days before their son was all for the school. This adolescent is so typical—idealistic, tending to see the possibilities as well as what is actual in life, easily angered and intolerant when things don't go the way they should. Adolescents do think differently than children. And their views on life and values may fluctuate even daily!

When faced with an unexpected crisis, they may lose the ability to see value in things. They become disillusioned, and when this occurs they tend to become cynical and even degrade others. This all leads to a resistance to change that makes counseling more difficult.[6]

Depression—a Neglected Topic

John's parents came to see me one day. They couldn't figure out what was wrong with their son. They said, "Ever since he lost his paper route, he's been a different person. It's a radical change. We ask him what's wrong and all we hear is 'nothing.' He mopes around and is tired all the time. Yet he sleeps twelve hours every night. He is so concerned about his acne. It's a preoccupation. And he seems so spacy! His mind is elsewhere."

Since teenagers are separating from their parents and endeavoring to establish their own identities, they will frequently experience the feeling of loss. John's loss of a paper route is a good example. And as we know, loss is at the basis of so much depression. Probably the most common loss of the adolescent is that of self-esteem.

Depression is actually more normal in this stage of life than in some others. Unfortunately, some of the depression of adolescence goes undiagnosed because the person is considered to be going through the "normal adolescent" throes of adjustment.

Depression in Younger Adolescents

Did you know there is a difference in the depression of adolescents thirteen through sixteen or seventeen as compared to older adolescents? Teenagers at the younger end of the scale have strong needs to deny self-critical attitudes. They avoid admitting personal concerns to others, even to a parent. Because of this, they fail to show or even experience the hopelessness, gloom, and self-deprecation seen in older teen and adult depression. They are also at a developmental stage in which, like children, they are tuned in less to thinking about something than doing something. They are more likely to express their depression through some outward behavior. Adults experience more introspective preoccupations.

How can you recognize depression in your teen? Some symptoms reflect the *inner state of being depressed.* There are three major symptoms to look for.

1. An excessive amount of fatigue. If your teenager complains of fatigue even after adequate rest, it could be he is suffering from depression that he can neither resolve nor express.

2. Hypochondriasis. Young adolescents are concerned about the ongoing changes that are normal for their age group. But when there is an excessive preoccupation with their bodily changes, it could reflect depression concerns about their own inadequacy. The young person has difficulty admitting this to himself and expressing it to others.

3. Inability to concentrate. This is probably the most com-

mon complaint that leads a teen to seek help. It may be seen in school performance and in other situations as well. The young adolescent often denies being apathetic or having anything on his mind that is bothering him. So don't be surprised when you ask "What's wrong?" and get a "Nothing's wrong" response. You may hear him say that his school work is going downhill. No matter how hard he studies, he cannot grasp the material or retain it. When you hear this, look for depression.

Sometimes a young person _tries to defend_ against the depression. One indication is being bored and restless. Keeping busy so you can keep your mind off things helps to avoid feeling depressed. And because the young teenager wants so much to avoid the feeling of depression, his activity level may become excessive. He seems to be driven and is very restless and bored. He alternates between a high level of interest in new activities and becoming quickly disenchanted with them.

Some adolescents frequently _dread being alone and look for constant companionship._ But they move from person to person searching for those who can give them time and attention. They want others for company who are not preoccupied with their own activity. Unfortunately, this frantic search leaves them with little time for their necessary functions. Sleep, chores, obligations, and school work receive the leftovers.

On the other hand, there are those who prefer to be alone. Why? Because being around others increases their fear of being rejected or abandoned. If a teenager takes this avenue of avoidance, he will pursue his own private activities with a tremendous intensity. He may have a higher interest in hobbies, pets, or anything that does not hold the potential for the rejection he so greatly fears.

Some teens _appeal for help._ This is usually evidenced by some kind of behavior that can include temper tantrums, running away, stealing, and a variety of other rebellious and antisocial acts.

Behaving in this way in an attempt to deal with depression has definite purposes for a teenager. When he is engaged in

some act that is exciting and new, it helps him avoid coming
to grips with what is bothering him. If the new behavior is
getting positive feedback from his peer group, his self-image
is bolstered. This behavior may also be manifested by a person
who does not have much impulse control. This in itself is a
cry for help. It is a message to others that he is in pain and
cannot handle his own life. His misbehavior is rarely carried
on secretly. The actions are usually public in some way and
conducted in such a manner that he is sure to be caught.[7]

Depression in Older Adolescents

Older adolescents tend to manifest their depression in ways
similar to those of adults. And yet they may still express depression indirectly.

Use of drugs may be an indication of depression. Yes, there
are a multitude of reasons for drug use, but some of them
are related to depression. Drugs serve several purposes. They
help the young person defend against being depressed. The
secrecy of obtaining illegal drugs adds a sense of excitement
to the person's life. And sharing the drug experience offers
acceptance in peer relationships.

Sexual misbehavior is also used to defend against being
depressed. The attention and the feeling of being needed and
wanted can overcome the feelings of sadness and being alone
and unloved.

Suicidal behavior is another indication. There has been significant rise in suicidal behavior and actual suicide with both
early and later adolescents. It could be because of depression,
or it could be tied in with other causes.

Loneliness along with its depression can be a key factor
for those who actually take their lives.

Alienation is another manifestation of depression. Older depressed adolescents may feel apathetic, out of touch with themselves and others. They do have some social contact with others
that gives the pretense of intimacy and belongingness. But
their peer group often reinforces depression because of who

they are. The young person avoids anything that might lead to a failure. He will not expose himself to any heartache. He is not a risk taker.

Why do adolescents become depressed? They have the same reasons as adults with the transitional struggles thrown in as well. Loss is a big factor. Rejection by others, losing an athletic event, having to wear braces at sixteen, are all real losses to an adolescent. So are fantasized losses. A fantasized loss is an unrealistic concern that causes the person to feel deprived. But there is nothing to justify this overconcern.[8]

There are other more serious losses. Grief is a part of loss. The type of grief will differ with the type of loss. When an adolescent loses a parent in death, if the relationship was close, there will be intense pain and anger at being left alone.

The death of a brother or sister brings a sense of loss. But there may also be some mixed feelings because of both positive and negative feelings that siblings have for one another.[9]

If an adolescent loses a friend in death, strong anxiety can result. Teenagers are aware that adults die. That seems normal. But the death of a peer is shocking and unnerving. They have to face their own mortality at an age when they are not prepared to do so.

Another loss that many face is in the divorce of their parents. Hank came in to see me and slumped on the chair. He said, "Who *can* you trust! I knew my folks had some problems, but divorce!? I can't believe it. I'm so ticked. I'm mad at Dad for what he did. But I'm just as mad at Mom for divorcing him." There is a loss of security and confidence in the future when this occurs. Anger at the parent who left usually is stronger and lasts longer than if the person had died. In death, the parent did not make a choice to leave. In divorce, the person does have a choice. So why did he or she leave? Guilt that the young person feels over the part he thinks he played in the divorce is strong and difficult to resolve. He does not blame himself for the divorce as much as younger children do. He may tend to spend more and more time away from home. Why? Home is no longer as safe and secure as it once was.

He may experience too much freedom and temptation that he is not yet equipped to handle. He may fear losing his friends now. If the person already has a tendency toward depression and withdrawal, it will be accentuated at this time.

Even a friend moving away brings a sense of loss. The pain suffered is as severe as rejection. The same sense of loss can occur when the person has to change schools or make any other type of move. All these can become a crisis.

Even normal changes present teenagers with a number of real losses and threats to their self-esteem. During this time they are expected to loosen their dependence upon their parents and they may do so. But some are tied closer to their parents than others and are hesitant to branch out on their own. Others break away as fast as they can. Now they are expected to receive emotional fulfillment from their peer group. But this is a far less secure and stable group than their parents. They are also expected to take responsibility for their futures and eventually the running of their lives. A key point for parents to remember is that the better a teenager is prepared to meet the challenges of adolescence, and change, the more likely he will be to avoid depression during this age.

What can you do as a parent? Listen and give empathy. Be available and supportive. If the young person is depressed and doesn't want to talk to you, ask if he would like to talk with someone else. Don't interpret this desire as a rejection of you as a person. Don't judge him and tell him to snap out of it. Teens need other trusted adults. Because of his tendency to focus on the negative and on unpleasant experiences, you may need to bring out the positive and attempt to reflect hopeful feelings. He will begin to feel more able to do this as you help him develop his strengths. He *has* solved problems before. Help him to remember how he accomplished his prior success. There are times to relate what has worked for you, but be sure this doesn't come across as advice or moralizing.

In working with your teen, it may be helpful to encourage him to write out his feelings. Many adolescents have difficulty expressing themselves face to face. Writing is private and helps a person uncover avoided or denied feelings. By writing, he can focus on his situation and feelings and become involved in looking at the feelings without embarrassment.

Sometimes writing letters, which are not sent, can help a young person work through his crisis feelings. For example, he might write to an absent parent or sibling who is no longer there because of divorce, separation, or death.

If an adolescent is disillusioned by a crisis, help him develop a support system, build his self-esteem, and discover meaning and purpose. How? Through empathy and listening and then problem solving. A young person receives support when you listen and understand his feelings. He wants his point of view to be heard and respected. As you listen to him, he in turn will listen to you as you offer your suggestions.

8

The Questions of Life

▽

The three questions most often asked by those in crisis are:

Why, God, why?

When, God, when?

Will I survive, God?

And of those three, the most common question of all is: Why? Why me? Why now? Why this? Why, God, why? You're not the first person in crisis to ask why and you won't be the last.

Sure, you've heard of Job, the man who lost it all—in just one day. One devastating crisis after another. His family, possessions, wealth, and health went. After several days of silence he began asking questions many of us ask.

"Why didn't I die at birth?"

"Why can't I die now?"

"Why has God done this to me?"

He threw the question, "Why?" at God sixteen times. Each time there was silence. And you know . . . silence was probably the best answer. I know that sounds strange but if God had given Job the answer to his question right away, would he have accepted it? Would you? Or would you argue and rail against His answer? You probably wouldn't understand God's reason at the time. By not having the answer, we have the opportunity to learn to live by faith.

The prophet Habakkuk asked a few questions in his day also. He was appalled by the suffering he saw. Listen to his complaint in Habakkuk 1:2–4.

> How long, O Lord, will I call for help, and Thou wilt not hear? I cry out to Thee, "Violence!" Yet Thou dost not save. *Why* dost Thou make me see iniquity, and cause me to look on wickedness? Yes, destruction and violence are before me; Strife exists and contention arises. Therefore, the law is ignored and justice is never upheld. For the wicked surround the righteous; Therefore, justice comes out perverted.

Although Habakkuk's "Why?" seemed to go unanswered, he eventually came to the place of confidence and hope:

> Though the fig tree should not blossom, And there be no fruit on the vines, Though the yield of the olive should fail, And the fields produce no food, Though the flock should be cut off from the fold, And there be no cattle in the stalls, Yet I will exult in the Lord, I will rejoice in the God of my salvation. (Habakkuk 3:17, 18)

In spite of everything falling apart, Habakkuk could rejoice in the Lord.

You too can come to the place of confidence and hope in your time of crisis. As you ask God why, also ask Him to help you come to the place where you can say, "In spite of . . . I will rejoice." Our goal is not just to cope but to celebrate no matter what!

God does not explain all suffering in the world or the meaning of each crisis that occurs. There is no clear explanation for some of the events that take place. God may not answer our "Why's" but He does tell us who to trust so that we can endure in the time of trouble.

A person who was experiencing a very upsetting crisis said, "You know, it feels as though I opened the doors of a blast furnace and the heat I'm experiencing is unbearable. I feel as though I'm melting away. There's going to be nothing left of me."

Sometimes life does feel that way. However, one of the greatest principles of handling life's crises is found in the statement of three men who literally faced a furnace. Listen to their solution.

> Nebuchadnezzar responded and said to them, "Is it true, Shadrach, Meshach and Abed-nego, that you do not serve my gods or worship the golden image that I have set up? Now if you are ready, at the moment you hear the sound of the horn, flute, lyre, trigon, psaltery, and the bagpipe, all kinds of music, to fall down and worship the image that I have made, very well. But if you will not worship, you will immediately be cast into the midst of a furnace of blazing fire; and what God is there who can deliver you out of my hands?" Shadrach, Meshach, and Abed-nego answered and said to the king, "O Nebuchadnezzar, we do not need to give you an answer concerning this. If it be so, our God whom we serve is able to deliver us from the furnace of blazing fire; and He will deliver us out of your hand, O king. But even if He does not, let it be known to you, O king, that we are not going to serve your gods or worship the golden image that you have set up." (Daniel 3:14–18)

Did you hear what they said! *"Even if He does not."* There it is—a statement of trust, of faith, and of living above and beyond the circumstances of life.

Each of us has our own dreams, desires, expectations, and hopes for our lives. If these come about then we say, "Everything is all right. I can handle life and I'm content. Now I can have the peace and stability I was looking for."

For many of us our faith is dependent upon getting God to do what we need. However, this is not the biblical pattern. It's all right to say, "Oh, I hope it turns out that way." "I hope the escrow doesn't fall through." "I hope he pulls through the operation." But we must also learn to say, "I hope . . . but even if it doesn't turn out that way, _it will be all right._"

Our stability in life begins when we can say these words, "even if He does not!" This is not a denial of life's problems. It is not rolling over and giving up or refusing to face life. It is a matter of surrendering to the wisdom of God and through this we gain strength.

Each of us has his own "fiery furnace" to face at one time or another. When such a crisis hits we must experience the normal emotional responses which are part of the healing process and then, with God's strength and stability, face the results. God does not always send in a rescue squad to get us out of the difficulty. (He doesn't always extinguish the fire in the furnace.) He does come in and say, "Let's go through this together." Things will be better tomorrow, but better from God's perspective. Saying, "even if He doesn't" means we are willing to leave the results to God.

God gives us the grace to live life. Grace is really God's assurance that life can be all right when everything in it is all wrong. It is the power to live life today as if things will be all right tomorrow. Lewis Smedes says it so well,

> Grace does not make everything right. Grace's trick is to show us that it is right for us to live; that it is truly good, wonderful even, for us to be breathing and feeling at the same time that everything clustering around us is wholly wretched. Grace is not a ticket to Fantasy Island; Fantasy Island is dreamy fiction. Grace is not a potion to charm life to our liking; charms are magic. Grace does not cure all our concerns, transform all our kids into winners, or send us all soaring into the high skies of sex and success. Grace is rather an amazing power to look earthy reality full in the face, see its sad and tragic edges, feel its cruel cuts, join in the primeval chorus against its outrageous unfairness, and yet feel in your deepest being that it is good and right for you to be alive on God's good earth.[1]

Crisis hurts but there is a positive side also. Months or years after a crisis, people admit the good that took place during or as a result of the situation.

Years ago the Flying Wallenda family experienced a tragedy while performing at a circus. As they attempted to perform a difficult formation on the high wire, two members of the family were killed and two were injured for life.

For awhile the Wallendas stopped their performances. They withdrew and became cautious which is a normal response. In time, however, they said they would get back up on the wire once again. In fact, they would perform the very act which led to tragedy.

The day came for the comeback. While people waited in the stands, the Wallendas successfully reconstructed their human pyramid on the high wire. After the performance reporters descended upon them. "Why did you try this act, after the tragedy a few days ago?" The senior member of the family replied immediately, "To be on the wire is life. All else is waiting."

The question is "How do you get back on the wire after a tragic fall?" [2]

Do you realize that your theology will affect how you respond to crisis? Your response to life's crises will be determined by your understanding of God.

We are people who usually put faith in formulas. We feel comfortable with predictability, regularity, and assurance. We want God to be like that and so we try to create Him in the image of what we want Him to be and what we want Him to do. However, you and I cannot predict what God will do. Paul reminds us of that in Romans 11:33. "O the depth of the riches both of the wisdom and knowledge of God! How unsearchable are His judgments, and His ways past finding out!"

God isn't busy elsewhere or noncaring. He is neither insensitive nor punitive. He is supreme, sovereign, loving, and sensitive.

I don't fully comprehend God. I, too, have unanswered questions about some of the events of my life. But all of life's trials, problems, crisis, and suffering occur by divine permission. Don Baker says:

God allows us to suffer. This may be the only solution to the problem that we will ever receive. Nothing can touch the Christian without having first received the permission of God. If I do not accept that statement, then I really do not believe that God is sovereign—and if I do not believe in His sovereignty, then I am helpless before all the forces of heaven and hell.[3]

God allows suffering for His purpose and for His reasons. He gives the permission. This should help us see God as the gracious controller of the universe. God is free to do as He desires . . . and He doesn't have to give us explanations nor share His reasons. He doesn't owe us. He has already given us His Son and His Holy Spirit who strengthens and guides us. We look at problems and crises and say "Why?" Jesus asks us to look at them and say "Why not?"

What God allows us to experience is for our growth. God has arranged the seasons of nature to produce growth and He arranges the experiences of the seasons of our lives for growth also. Some days bring sunshine and some bring storms. Both are necessary. He knows the amount of pressure that we can handle. First Corinthians 10:13 tells us He will, ". . . not let you be tempted beyond what you can bear." But He does let us be tempted, feel pain, and experience suffering. He gives us not always what we think we need or want but what will produce growth.

A woman came to me for counseling sometime ago. She was in the midst of a crisis and she was upset because a friend had suggested that she thank God for the problems she was experiencing.

"I can't believe she'd say that," the woman exclaimed. "That's ridiculous! It's insensitive! How can I thank God for being hurt?" She continued to vent her frustration.

After awhile I said, "I wonder what she meant by her comment."

"What do you mean?" she replied.

"Well, did she mean to thank God for this specific crisis as though it were good in and of itself—or to thank God for using this situation so that you can change and grow? Could that be it?"

"Well . . . I don't know," she ventured.

"I know it hurts and your family wishes it had never occurred," I said, "But it did. So the past can't be changed and you feel out of control. Perhaps you can't change what happens in the future but you can control your response to whatever occurs. It's just something to think about."

She did think about it and in time she came to the place of thanking God for being with her and allowing her this time of growth.

"One day I thought about the choices I had," she said. "I could depend on God, thank Him and praise Him and allow Him to work through me. This didn't seem so bad when I considered the alternative!"

What kind of growth can we expect? Lloyd Ogilvie suggests some of the things we can learn as we go through the difficult times in life which he calls valleys:

> First, it has been in the valleys of waiting for answers to my prayers that I have made the greatest strides in growing in the Lord's grace.
> Second, it's usually in retrospect, after the strenuous period is over, that I can look back with gratitude for what I've received of the Lord Himself. I wouldn't trade the deeper trust and confidence I experienced from the valley for a smooth and trouble-free life.
> Third, I long to be able to remember what the tough times provide in my relationship with the Lord, so that when new valleys occur, my first reaction will be to thank and praise the Lord in advance for what is going to happen in and through me as a result of what happens to me. I really want my first thought to be, "Lord, I know You didn't send this, but You have allowed it and will use it as a part of working all things together for good. I trust You completely, Lord!"[4]

This attitude doesn't negate the turmoil of a crisis. When we are in crisis we feel like the disciples adrift in that small boat during the storm on the Sea of Galilee. The waves throw us about and just as we get our legs under us, we're hit from another direction. They struggled on the Sea of Galilee and we struggle on the sea of life. All of us are afraid of capsizing. All we see are the waves which seem to grow each moment. We're afraid. Fear is the strong emotion of a crisis. However, Jesus came to the disciples and He comes to us today with the same message, "It is I; do not be afraid" (John 6:20). Remember the words of the song, "Here comes Jesus, walking on the water, He'll lift you up . . ."?

> Here comes Jesus, See Him walking on the water,
> He'll lift you up and He'll help you to stand;
> Oh, here comes Jesus, He's the Master of the waves that roll,
> Here comes Jesus, He'll save your soul.
>
> Here comes Jesus, See Him walking on the water,
> He'll lift you up and He'll help you to stand;
> Oh, here comes Jesus, He's the Master of the waves that roll,
> Here comes Jesus, He'll make you whole.[5]

We ask God, "Where are You?" But He is there in the midst of the crisis. We ask Him, "When? When will You answer?" As the psalmist cried, "How long, O Lord? Wilt Thou forget me forever? How long wilt Thou hide Thy face from me? How long shall I take counsel in my soul, having sorrow in my heart all the day? How long will my enemy be exalted over me?" (Psalm 13:1-2). We want Him to act according to our time table but the Scripture says, "Be still before the Lord and wait patiently for Him" (Psalm 37:7). We become restless in waiting. And to block out the pain of waiting, we are often driven into frantic activity. This does not help, however, but resting before the Lord does.

> Often waiting is a time of darkening clouds. Our skies do not lighten. Instead, everything seems to become even more grim.
> Yet the darkening of our skies may forecast the dawn. It

is in the gathering folds of deepening shadows that God's hidden work for us takes place. The present, no matter how painful, is of utmost importance.

Somewhere, where our eyes cannot see and our ears are unable to hear, God is. And God is at work.[6]

You may not feel that God is doing anything! Why? Because we want results *now*. The instant solution philosophy of our society often invades a proper perspective of God. We complain about waiting for a few weeks or days but to God a day is as a thousand years and a thousand years an instant. God works in hidden ways even when you and I are totally frustrated by His apparent lack of response. We are just unaware that He is active. Hear the words of Isaiah for the people then and us now.

> Since ancient times no one has heard,
>   no ear has perceived,
> no eye has seen any God besides you,
>   who acts on behalf of those who wait for him.
> You come to the help of those who gladly do right,
>   who remember your ways. (Isaiah 64:4–5 NIV).

God has a reason for everything He does and a time table for when He does it. " 'For I know the plans I have for you,' declares the Lord, 'plans to prosper you and not to harm you, plans to give you hope and a future' " (Jeremiah 29:11 NIV). Give yourself permission not to know what, not to know how, and not to know when. Even though you feel adrift on the turbulent ocean, God is holding you and knows the direction of your drift. Giving yourself permission to wait can give you hope. It is all right for God to ask us to wait for weeks and months and even years. During that time when we do not receive the answer and/or solution we think we need, He gives us His presence. "But I trust in you, O Lord; I say, 'You are my God.' My times are in your hands" (Psalm 31:14–15 NIV).

Who Are the Survivors?

There are some individuals who survive crisis and move ahead with their lives. Others become anchored in the tragedy and pain and their growth is stunted. Some adults never recover from a miscarriage, a child on drugs, a financial reversal, or a disappointing love relationship. Others recover and move on with productive lives in spite of a divorce, becoming a quadreplegic, discovering a child is gay, or having a terminal illness.

What is the difference? Who are the survivors?

Those who are able to survive a tragedy give credit to one person who ministered to them, stood by them, and gave them hope.

To help survive a crisis, you need the support of a friend. A friend helps us cope with our fears. Often in a crisis, we experience the fear of abandonment but the presence of a friend reduces this. A friendship affirms that we won't be abandoned. A friend helps to break the hold of feelings of helplessness and hopelessness. Dr. Elton Mayo says, "One friend, one person who is truly understanding, who takes the trouble to listen to us as we consider our problem, can change our whole outlook on the world."[7]

A second characteristic of those who survive a crisis is the ability to understand the extent of their loss. To recover, you need to fully experience the loss. Talking over the crisis and letting tears drain is necessary. Denying the crisis and the depth of it delays the recovery. Facing the crisis helps us remember what we have lost but promotes healing.

"Our pain and hurt do not go out the door of our life at one point in time. It is more of a slow drainage. And as there are seasons during the year, there are seasons of drainage. There is a season of sadness, a season of anger, a season of tranquility, a season of hope. But these seasons do not always follow sequentially in a crisis. Winter, spring and summer can be jumbled together. One morning you feel that hope and sunlight have entered your life again. But the next day, the storm is back. We smile one minute and cry the next."[8]

A third characteristic of survivors is that they stop blaming themselves and living with guilt. Too often in a crisis we ask "If only . . ." again and again, and "What have I done to deserve this?" Guilt weakens us and delays recovery more than any other factor. Our self-talk tends to become negative and we must make a conscious effort to be objective and self-affirming. Even when we are responsible for the occurrence, we must forgive ourselves. Because of our acceptance and forgiveness by God, we *can* forgive ourselves.

Survivors are those who have a purpose in life. They do not live in the past nor focus on the negatives. In spite of the loss and the crisis they are willing to search out the positives which do exist in their lives. Expecting something more from life helps the recovery process. What is this element of expectation? Hope![9]

There is yet a final characteristic of those who not only survive but move forward as stronger individuals. It is the ability to develop a biblical perspective on life.

"Consider it all joy, my brethren, when you encounter various trials, knowing that the testing [or trying] of your faith produces endurance" (James 1:2–3). It's easy to read a passage like this and say, "Well, that's fine." It is another thing, however, to put it into practice.

What does the word *consider* actually mean? It refers to an internal attitude of the heart or the mind that allows the trial and circumstance of life to affect us adversely or beneficially. Another way James 1:2 might be translated is: "Make up your mind to regard adversity as something to welcome or be glad about."

You have the power to decide what your attitude will be. You can approach it and say: "That's terrible. Totally upsetting. That is the last thing I wanted for my life. Why did it have to happen now? Why me?"

The other way of "considering" the same difficulty is to say: "It's not what I wanted or expected, but it's here. There are going to be some difficult times, but how can I make the best of them?" Don't ever deny the pain or the hurt that you might have to go through, but always ask, "What can I learn

102

from it? How can I grow through this? How can it be used for God's glory?"

The verb tense used in the word _consider_ indicates a decisiveness of action. It's not an attitude of resignation—"Well, I'll just give up. I'm just stuck with this problem. That's the way life is." If you resign yourself, you will sit back and not put forth any effort. The verb tense actually indicates that you will have to go against your natural inclination to see the trial as a negative force. There will be some moments when you won't see it like that at all, and then you'll have to remind yourself: "No, I think there is a better way of responding to this. Lord, I really want You to help me see it from a different perspective." And then your mind will shift to a more constructive response. This often takes a lot of work on your part.

God created us with both the capacity and the freedom to determine how we will respond to those unexpected incidents that life brings our way. You may honestly wish that a certain event had never occurred. But you cannot change the fact.

During the time of crisis as well as all the other times of life, our stability comes from our Lord. God's Word says: "Now to Him who is able to establish you according to my gospel and the preaching of Jesus Christ, according to the revelation of the mystery which has been kept secret for long ages past" (Romans 16:25).

"Then he said to them, 'Go, eat of the fat, drink of the sweet, and send portions to him who has nothing prepared; for this day is holy to our Lord. Do not be grieved, for the joy of the Lord is your strength' " (Nehemiah 8:10).

"And He shall be the stability of your times, a wealth of salvation, wisdom, and knowledge; the fear of the Lord is his treasure" (Isaiah 33:6).

Sure it hurts, but what can you do? What a tragedy if there is no way out.

But there is a way out. This is the message of the Bible. _You can find courage for crisis living!_ You can take it! Crisis is the overture. Hurt is the introduction. Courage is the climax, and God is the ultimate resource.

This is the message of Job: "Though he [God] slay me,

yet will I trust in him. . ." (Job 13:15 KJV). This was the message of David: "Yea, though I walk through the valley of the shadow of death, I will fear no evil: for thou art with me; thy rod and thy staff they comfort me" (Psalm 23:4 KJV). This was the message of Isaiah: "Thou wilt keep him in perfect peace, whose mind is stayed on thee: because he trusteth in thee" (Isaiah 26:3 KJV). This was the message of Paul: "For I am persuaded, that neither death, nor life, nor angels, nor principalities, nor powers, nor things present, nor things to come, Nor height, nor depth, nor any other creature, shall be able to separate us from the love of God, which is in Christ Jesus our Lord" (Romans 8:38, 39 KJV).

The three questions to ask in the middle of a crisis are:

What can I learn from this?

How can I grow through this?

How can God be glorified through this?

When you and I are afflicted and faint, we are invited to pour out our laments to the Lord. Gradually, as we do, the Holy Spirit will shift the focus of our awareness. He will lead us to remember the nature of the one to whom we speak. Remembering the Lord, our perspective will gradually change. The surging emotions will begin to still. The fears will quiet; the turbulence will give way to peace. As we remember who God is, our prayer will express trust, and we too will find ourselves moved to praise.[10]

Part II

Creating a Positive, Controlled Crisis

9

Creating a Constructive Crisis

▽

Risky! That is the only way to describe the next four chapters. What I am about to suggest is *risky*. Why? Because in many ways it is different from what is suggested in other books. Because it could be misused, misunderstood, misapplied, and not bring about the results you desire. There is no guarantee but I feel this path of action is worth considering. What I want to suggest is this: Many crisis situations which we experience would not have to occur if we took charge of the situation early on and created a positive, controlled crisis ourselves! Does that sound shocking, unchristian, radical? It may at first, but look again at two key words: *positive* and *controlled*. A positive, controlled crisis can be the catalyst to change an intolerable situation.

Many times we inadvertently bring about crisis or contribute to one by the way we respond in certain situations. We feel that we are victims but in reality we may have been contributing victims. How? By allowing the problem to continue through our passivity, by behaving and responding in ways which are predictable and actually reinforce the problem, or by actually believing that we may deserve what the other individual is doing to us. There are other ways also that we contribute to a problem, but focusing on the why is not the solution. Learning to respond in a *new way* can bring about significant change.

I work with many individuals and couples who are experiencing a marital or family crisis. Often I am left with the feeling, "This didn't have to happen if someone had taken charge through a different approach and shocked the other person involved." It may not have taken an all-out crisis to bring about change. It could have been a confrontation or a new attention-getting or shocking response with love and concern.

Over the years I have tended sometimes to work too much and become overly involved. I have improved somewhat during the last few years but sometimes I still take on too much. On a few occasions my wife, Joyce, has confronted me with this fact. But the last time she did so, she really got my attention. In a direct, caring, loving manner she said, "Norm, I feel you are doing entirely too much and I would rather you slow down by yourself instead of slowing down because of a heart attack or dropping dead." That was all she said but I heard her!

To reinforce what I am trying to say, I would like you to meet a couple who experienced a marital crisis. Their story is told in their own words and comes from their book, *Rekindled.* Here is what happened:

> "I just don't care anymore," she said, so quietly he almost couldn't hear her. Almost. "I hate this marriage. It's boring me to death." He heard that as if she'd screamed it in his ear, yet she spoke just above a whisper, staring at the floor. Pat leaned close to look in her face, realizing that she meant it, that her eyes and even her color signaled something in her he had never encountered. This wasn't something he could apologize away, something he could patch up. . . .[1]

For Pat and Jill Williams, Sunday, 19 December 1982 has come to be known as D-day in their marriage. It was the day of the bomb, the surprise attack, the confrontation that would make or break their ten-year marriage.

Ironically, the D-day was not planned. Pat, forty-two, was oblivious to the despair that had driven his thirty-three-year-old wife to the brink. She had long since resigned from the fight. No more whining, begging, shouting, nagging. She was finished, exiled to a bad marriage with a man who thought she was happy. Or should be.

Pat hadn't even really noticed that her tactics had changed. Perhaps the few months leading to the explosion were more peaceful than before. But that was only a relief. Maybe his young wife had merely matured, grown up, quit being so demanding, so petty, so selfish.

All he knew was that things were quieter around the house than they had been in a long time. He no longer had to defend himself from accusations, from charges that he didn't care, didn't listen, didn't praise her in public, didn't make her a priority. Maybe she seemed a little sullen lately—and there was some irrational behavior that troubled him, but basically, things were calm, and that was good.

It was a typical Sunday morning after a Philadelphia 76ers basketball game the night before. Though for some reason Jill had stopped watching the games, Pat as 76ers vice-president and general manager, of course, always did. He got to bed late at their suburban New Jersey home after watching the Sixers play the Bullets on TV from Washington. He and Jill would skip Sunday school in the morning and take their children Jimmy, eight, Bobby, five, and Karyn, three, to church at eleven.

Pat had gone to bed unhappy. The Sixers had lost to the Washington Bullets, and three of his guards had been all but mugged by illegal moves from a Bullets agitator. Pat was angry about that and depressed by the loss.

Never down for long, by morning Pat was up and active, doing his daily Bible study and memorizing his one-a-day verse to fulfill a life commitment. He read, studied, memorized, showered and shaved, dressed, and was ready to go.

Jill, however, having as usual to get herself and three children ready, was running behind. She had fixed breakfast and cleared the table and put dinner in the oven, but despite the extra time afforded the family by skipping Sunday school, by a few minutes before eleven it was obvious they were going to be late. Again.

Jill had supervised the dressing and feeding of the boys and little Karyn. Now, as she stood before the mirror hurriedly applying her makeup, first one, then another came with a shoelace that had come untied or a shock of hair that wouldn't be combed into submission. "Ask your father, please. Pat! Would you help, please?"

Not volunteering, never offering, but always willing to help, "If you'd just ask me," he tied their shoes and dragged a comb through their hair as Jill hurried to dig coats out of the closet. She hated being late, but it had been ages since they were on time.

Pat remembers that he often helped with the kids before and after church. Jill's impression is that he only helped when she forced the issue. In his mind, "I wasn't just sitting there doing nothing." In her memory, he either sat in the car or stood waiting by the door.

At the office, Pat was always on time, everything was on schedule, things were precise. At home, he felt it was his responsibility to keep things moving, to keep people on track. Not so much by sharing the work load, but by motivating. Quick with a nickname, always ready with a fast quip, Pat was never at a loss for words. Often encouraging, frequently not.

His shoe-tying and hair-combing tasks accomplished, he pored over the paper, exposing box-score details to his photographic memory. Twice, as Jill scurried past, he took gentle—he thought—shots at her. "Hope you sing the hymns this morning." Sometimes she did, sometimes she didn't. Lately, she hadn't.

She ignored him. He hadn't thought much about why he said it. Looking back, he thinks he was only trying to keep her moving, get her motivated, get her out the door so they could all get to church.

Jill hurried past again. She had quickly regained her figure after having Karyn, and she looked as good as she had in years. Indeed, she could have worn the same clothes she wore in 1972 when she won the talent (violin) and bathing-suit competitions on her way to being first runner-up to Miss Illinois.

She had always dressed well, and her dark hair and eyes and clear complexion set off perfect, gleaming teeth. A mention of her beauty from Pat would have stopped her in her tracks, made her day, maybe put a smile on her face. Instead, despite the natural beauty, there was a set to the jaw, a weariness in the eyes, a stiffness in the gait. "Haven't seen you studying your Bible lately," he called after her.

She turned to glare at him but had neither the time nor the energy to say what she thought. He glanced up briefly, just long enough to realize he had cut her deeply with that remark. "It was as if her lights went out," he recalls. He got the icy, silent treatment for the rest of the morning.

They arrived ten minutes late to their little house of worship. Often Jill had concerned Pat by not singing out during congregational hymns, but this time she didn't sing at all. Didn't open her mouth.

Jill had perfected the silent treatment over the years to where she could make it perfectly clear to Pat that he was in the doghouse, while charming the socks off her friends and co-parishioners. And even though this would be a day unlike any other day in their marriage, she didn't know that yet. And the routine was the same—Pat got the ice; everyone else got the warm fuzzies.

On the way out it was a smile and a "Hi, hello, how are you?" for everyone, and Pat and Jill gradually lost contact with each other. Pat wanted to go home. He was hungry, there were games to watch on television, and he figured he'd probably have to have a little fence-mending session with Jill.

There had been a few of those over the years. When he couldn't deflect the badgering or the sullenness or the crying or the silence, he would sit her down to find out what was wrong, apologize for whatever unintentional thing he had said or done, and try to get on with life. If she wasn't better on the way home, if things didn't loosen up a little in the car, it was apparent he was going to have to try to smooth things over. It might even require taking her to dinner some night soon. Anything to keep the peace and get things back to normal. Normal was fine with Pat. Normal was killing Jill.

He sat in the car in the parking lot, nodding and waving to friends, not wanting to be responsible for getting home any later than necessary. Jill was rounding up all three kids, a chore she knew by now was expected of her. But if there had been any possibility of a thaw in her mood, it was obliterated when she found Pat waiting impatiently in the car while she herded the kids into the back seat.

On the way home, Pat attempted a few forays into the wall she had erected. She didn't look at him. She answered with as few words as possible. She pretended to be preoccupied with the children.

Their normal course on Sunday was to eat out so they could get home and get Karyn down for a nap. As it happened, however, Jill had prepared a lunch that day. It was during lunch when Pat realized that, indeed, this was a spat which needed patching up. She was so cold and quiet during the meal, he recalls, "It was as if she wasn't a factor at all."

She put Karyn down for her nap and returned to the kitchen to clean up. Pat clapped Jimmy on the shoulder. "Why don't you and Bobby go play in the family room while I talk to Mother."

Jill felt a flutter in the pit of her stomach as Jimmy and Bobby disappeared and Pat led her to the living room. He had said he wanted to talk to her with such an ominous finality that she wondered if she would be able to fake her way out of a confrontation as she so often did. Hiding her fear and discomfort, she immediately threw on a frustrated, impatient face. She wanted him to know she was wishing he'd get on with it so she could finish in the kitchen and get a nap before her concert that night at church.

Pat was convinced his two verbal shots that morning had hurt her, and he merely wanted to apologize to reestablish peace in the home. It was bad enough that he had to go to the 76ers Christmas party that night and would miss her concert; that made it difficult for both of them, having to make excuses for each other. He didn't need another rift between them.

Jill pulled her hand away from his and headed for the couch directly across from the green and white love seat where he was about to sit. She didn't want to be next to him, but he quickly rose and guided her, a hand on each shoulder, to sit with him. She pressed her lips tight and wouldn't look at him.

"Now, Jill, what's wrong?"

She shook her head and spoke softly, "Nothing."

A meaningless, typical response to which Pat could have responded a hundred different ways. He could have stood and embraced her and said, "Jill, that's wonderful. I was afraid you were upset because of what I said this morning. Forgive me and let's go on." He could have said, "Fine, if you aren't going to tell me, then there's nothing I can do about it."

But he felt he had caused the problem; it was a little spat, and he wanted to take care of it, to handle it properly. "No," he said, "this time I'm not going to accept 'nothing.' Something's been bothering you for hours and I want you to tell me what it is."

Inwardly, Jill flinched. "Nothing," she repeated, desperate to keep from having to tell the whole truth. Because this time it wasn't something he'd said or done, an argument, an oversight, an offense. It was everything, and it had been building for the last two months on a foundation that had been poured the day they were married. She stood to leave, but he stopped her.

"Jill, I want you to tell me. We're going to sit here and get this straight if it takes all night."

"What do you mean? Why?"

"Listen, you're not singing in church, you're not having your devotions, you're snapping at the kids. Tell me what's wrong."

Pat still thought that if he could get the reason out of her, it would concern his unkind remarks that morning. He and Jill still cringe at the thought that he could have let her off the hook by suggesting that or by letting her head back to the kitchen insisting nothing was wrong.

Jill hadn't planned to say what she said next. It surprised her as much as it did Pat, but it didn't shock her, didn't cut her to the bone the way it did him. Her shocking and cutting had come gradually over the years. He was getting his all at once.

"I just don't care anymore," she said, so quietly he almost couldn't hear her. Almost. "I hate this marriage. It's boring me to death." He heard that as if she'd screamed it in his ear, yet she spoke just above a whisper, staring at the floor. Pat leaned close to look in her face, realizing that she meant it, that her eyes and even her color signaled something in her he had never encountered. This wasn't something he could apologize away, something he could patch up with a babysitter and a dinner in Philly.

"I give up," she managed.

"Jill, I'm sorry. I didn't mean to upset you with what I said this morning. I apologize for that." But he could tell, as she waved him off with a flick of her hand, that it went much deeper.

"I don't even know if I love you anymore. I don't even know if I ever loved you."

Pat felt as if his heart had stopped. "Really, Jill?" he said, his throat tight. "What can I do? What can we do?"

Jill began a soft litany of the countless complaints she had registered for so many years, never having felt she had really gotten his attention long enough to get any response. He looked at her sadly and she wondered if he was finally hearing her for the first time.

If he had only been listening all those years, the charges echoing in his mind wouldn't have come as revelations now:

You don't really care about this marriage.

Why should I try to be a good wife? You never notice anything anyway.

We never do anything together unless it's something you want to do.

You never share anything with me, your work, your Bible study, your dreams, your goals.

Why can't you remember the little things, the special days unless I circle them in red on the calendar?

You talk to me like I'm a Philadelphia sportswriter.

Couldn't you even come home a little early just to be with me? Or come and pick me up and take me to the game instead of leaving me to find my own way there with friends?

You never hold my hand anymore. You never touch me unless you want something more.

You never say nice things to me in front of people.

You're okay with the kids only after I've asked you five or six times.

You never act as if my words are important. You never really listen. You either interrupt or don't let me talk at all when we're with other people.

I don't want things. I want you. Don't give me crumbs. I want the real thing. You've never made a one hundred percent commitment to me. You've never really given me you.

Pat was listening now. For years she had suggested marriage seminars and marriage books, but he had really not seen the need. To him, his marriage was fine. Sure, his wife was a little moody at times, hard to please, maybe a little spoiled. But they always worked it out. She was a rock, always there when he needed her, running a good house, raising the kids, often singing at his speaking engagements. Until that moment, when Jill finally surprised herself by letting it all tumble out, Pat Williams thought he had a great marriage. Even an ideal one.

"Jill, how can you say you don't love me? I love _you._ "

"I didn't really know you when we got married," she said, if anything even more quietly now. "I didn't really know you as a person. It was fairly quick. Maybe I made a mistake. How do I know that I didn't?"

"I know _I_ didn't," Pat said, desperate to keep her talking.

"I know you're the girl God picked out for me."

It was as if she hadn't heard him. "I'm not going to leave because the kids would be devastated. I'll stick around. I know as a Christian that divorce isn't an option. Maybe I should go away for a while."

"Do you think that would help? If you think that would help, that would be fine. Do what you have to do to get your act together, Jill, because we're going to work this out. Should we talk to someone?"

"Who would we talk to, Pat? Anyone around here thinks we're Mr. and Mrs. Joe Christian with our whole thing together."

"Should we talk to someone we don't know, who doesn't know us?"

"I don't even want to think about it."

"We have to think about it. We have to do something."

"Don't worry, I won't leave you. I'll cook your meals and wash your clothes and take care of the kids. But I can't enjoy being with you anymore. I've given up."

"What do you mean, you've given up?"

"I can't seem to get you to spend time with me or respond to me, but I know biblically I have to stay with you, so I'll stay. I can't promise any emotion. Don't expect any response or any real feeling from me, because I don't have any left."

Pat was eager to talk about arranging a vacation for her, anything to help, anything to keep her talking, anything to get her to look at him, to speak up, to stay there. But she had talked enough, and all she could think of was getting upstairs for a nap. "Think about where you might like to go to get away for awhile," he said. "Or who we might talk to."

She nodded without enthusiasm and heaved a heavy sigh. "I'm very tired. I need a nap before I sing tonight." And she trudged upstairs alone, leaving Pat in shock. He realized as he sat there that he had just seen his wife die emotionally. It was absolutely the most frightening thing he'd ever seen in his life.

She wanted out, she didn't care, she wasn't sure she loved

him. That hurt. Part of him still wished he hadn't said what he'd said that morning, but down deep he knew it went much further and deeper than that. He felt totally rejected and could only hope she'd made her statements in anger and that she didn't really mean them. He hoped that after her nap, she'd feel better.

For Jill's part, all she knew was that she had finally gotten his attention, but she sincerely didn't care anymore. She was relieved to have finally quit living the lie, at least in front of Pat. That night, she would live it before her own congregation, smiling and singing Christmas songs. She hated being a phony, so she chose only general songs that didn't hit too close to home. That she could even survive the concert in the mental and emotional state she was in was miraculous in itself.

Pat had checked in on the children and then ran hard and long that afternoon while Jill napped. The exercise in the frigid winter air was invigorating, but he was unable to run off his fear, his sense of dread, of failure, of rejection. He had been rocked to the core, and he had no idea what he was going to do.

Jill was no better after her nap. She couldn't look at him, wouldn't talk to him, wouldn't respond to his good-by peck as he headed for the Christmas party. Usually the life of such parties, as one of the bosses and a nationally known humorist, Pat was only able to sleepwalk through the niceties. He was distracted, nervous, hollow.

He felt the need to hurry home on this snowy night. Maybe after her concert Jill would be in a better mood to talk. She might accept his sincere apology, and maybe take back some of the things she had said.

It wasn't terribly late when he arrived home. But the house was dark. The old hardwood floors squeaked and groaned. She had to know he was there. But when he entered the bedroom, there was no response. Could she be sound asleep? It appeared so. He undressed on the verge of tears.

One thing the Philadelphia 76ers vice-president and general manager had never had trouble doing was falling asleep. Anyone who ever knew him in any capacity said he was one of the busiest, most fast-paced, hard-driving executives they'd ever seen, totally committed, even obsessed with every area of life. He worked hard and long and he slept good and sound.

But not this night. He slid between the sheets that had never seemed icier and let his eyes grow accustomed to the dark. Jill slept with her back to him. He gently rested his hand on her side, just above her hip, and held his breath to see if he could detect any change in her breathing. She didn't stir. He rolled to his back, his hands behind his head, and stared wide-eyed at the ceiling in the darkness.

He needed his sleep. The holidays were a busy time in the 76ers office. But his well-ordered and disciplined life was unraveling all at once. To Jill it may have been happening for years. For Pat, the trauma was only hours old.

He and Jill were coming up on their unmerriest Christmas ever. What had he done? Where had he failed? How could this ever have happened?

Jill's feelings had been dying for years. Telling Pat how she felt created the crisis that was needed. Fortunately, she was committed to marriage. Many women in her situation would have opted for divorce. Pat worked to win back Jill's love but it didn't happen quickly. It took over two years.

I have heard this story many times with variations. Many marriages contain one person who is eagerly working on building closeness and intimacy, seeking improvement. But their spouse is resistant to change, doesn't see anything wrong with the marriage, and doesn't care. The marriage continues in this fashion for twelve or fifteen years until the eager person becomes weary and disheartened. He or she has nothing left to give and becomes indifferent, perhaps even leaving the marriage.

Many divorces, separations, children going out of control, and in-law problems do not have to occur if the concerned individuals will respond in a new manner. This new approach can take the form of unpredictable behavior, confrontation, or a controlled, positive crisis. If you are interested in learning how, please read on.

10

Why Should a Person Change?

▽

The desire to help those we care about to change and grow is natural. Some of the changes we seek, especially in family relationships, are minor—ranging from misbehavior on the part of a child to sloppiness and irresponsibility on the part of a spouse. Some are major including abuse, infidelity, workaholism, and so on. If you have a family relationship which is positive, healthy, and growing, praise God! This section of the book is probably not for you, but perhaps you could pass it on to someone in need. For there are many people who desperately want change to occur. A husband wants his wife to change, a parent wants her child to change, a friend wants a close friend to change.

People are strange. For years they search for just the right person to be their mate—someone who is attractive, loving, considerate, and all those other qualities they hold dear. At last they find the right one and hasten to tie the knot. Then are they satisfied? Well, not exactly. Reforming tendencies soon emerge and the struggle begins.[1]

Is it abnormal to want to change another person? Do all

married couples consider changing their relationship and their partner? Yes, indeed, at least in some ways seeking change is a normal response when people are committed to one another. Too often couples do not realize that desiring change in each other *can* be an act of caring.

Why do we want another person to change? Often our reasons are indicated in statements such as the following:

"I don't like what he/she does."

"It creates more work for me."

"It's for his own good."

"I have to complete the work his parents never finished."

"I just want to improve our relationship."

"What he/she is doing is dangerous!"

"I can't stand that behavior any more."

"I need affirmation."

What change do you have in mind for someone you care about? Can you identify from the list above your reasons for wanting the change?

Let's look at the last reason in more detail. Underlying many of the reasons to change another is our own need to belong, to be accepted, to be loved, to feel we are special to another person. Affirmation is a major need. Sometimes original feelings of affirmation have diminished. We then look for a change in the relationship to renew those lost feelings. We want to recapture good feelings about ourselves. Thus we want our spouse to change in some way so things can again "be the way they once were." Actually renewed affirmation underlies many of our reasons from "It's for his own good," to "I can't stand it any more."

A wife may want to recapture the first year of marriage: "I want him to take the afternoon off once a week as he did twenty years ago. We would go for a walk or ride bikes or lie on the floor in front of the fireplace and read or talk. I want him to court me again. What's wrong with that?"

There are many who feel they have never received sufficient affirmation. Their cry is for *more!* Our need for positive responses from others will vary according to our background and self-esteem. When we want more it may mean quality or a different approach. A wife said, "My husband is attractive. He touches me, compliments me now and then, but often I hint for the compliments. I would like him to think for himself and create new compliments. I want to be loved and pursued ten times the amount I am now. In fact, I'd settle for a fifty percent increase! And I don't want to tell him how to do it either!"

A different expression of affirmation of love may be needed if we feel our spouse has taken us for granted or our relationship has become routine. If a spouse affirms us in the same old ways, it is not enough. His or her love needs to be expressed in some new ways. Why? So that we are convinced of our spouse's sincerity. "My wife is very loving and affirming. But she is so predictable. I like all that she does but it's almost like she's been programmed a certain way. I want some surprises. I'd like her to say new things to me, to be different in her sexual responses too. I guess I should be satisfied. So many men don't receive what I do, and yet. . . ."

Well, what about asking for change? Can the Word of God shed any light on this?

How does the biblical mandate to exhort one another or encourage one another apply to the desire for change? Let's look at some examples from the Word of God (italics have been added).

"And when [Apollos] wished to cross to Achaia [most of Greece], the brethren wrote to the disciples there, *urging and encouraging* them to accept and welcome him heartily" (Acts 18:27 AMP).

"I *entreat* and *advise* Euodia and I entreat and advise Syntyche to agree and to work in harmony in the Lord" (Philippians 4:2 AMP).

"Let the word [spoken by] the Christ, the Messiah, have its home [in your hearts and minds] and dwell in you in [all its] richness, as you *teach* and *admonish* and *train* one another in all insight and intelligence and wisdom [in spiritual things, and sing] psalms and hymns and spiritual songs, making melody to God with [His] grace in your hearts" (Colossians 3:16 AMP).

"But we *beseech* and *earnestly exhort* all you, brethren, that you excel [in this matter] more and more" (1 Thessalonians 4:10 AMP).

"Therefore *encourage* [admonish, exhort] one another and *edify*—strengthen and build up—one another, just as you are doing" (1 Thessalonians 5:11 AMP).

Who determines what we are to exhort another person to do? Who determines what we are to teach another or encourage another person to do?

The word *exhort* in these passages means to urge one to pursue some course of conduct. It is always looking to the future. Exhorting one another is a threefold ministry in which one believer *urges* another to action in terms of applying scriptural truth, *encourages* the person with scriptural truth, and *comforts* the person through the application of Scripture. *Encourage* is to urge forward or persuade in Acts 18:27. In 1 Thessalonians 5:11 it means to stimulate another to the ordinary duties of life. Therefore, what are we to exhort another person to do?

To answer this you need to look at your motives for change. When you begin to understand what your motives really are, you may discover that it isn't really necessary for the other person to change. Perhaps your needs can be fulfilled in other ways which allow the person not to have to change. If you can discover why you want them to change, you may discover that you really want change in your own life. The key is to understand your own motives.

On the other hand, you may have some very good reasons for wanting the person to change. There may be a serious deficiency in the relationship, an irresponsible behavior which creates additional work, or a serious threat to the entire family.

What are the means by which you can attempt to bring about change? Let me list both the good and the bad and we'll go from there.

You can do the following:

1. Become irate and threaten.
2. Beg.
3. Plead.
4. Cry.
5. Punish and withhold.
6. Request.
7. Confront.
8. Create a positive shock.
9. Create a positive, controlled, well-thought-out crisis.
10. Go for counseling by yourself.
11. Go for counseling with the other person.

Counseling can be very beneficial, especially if both individuals are willing to work toward change. But when one person is oblivious to the problem, doesn't care, and is headed in another direction, a different approach is needed. Loving and caring for the other individual from a biblical basis is essential. But love also contains concern, discipline, confrontation, and exhortation. There are times in all our lives when we need to be admonished to more mature behavior, when the situation calls for direct action to bring about positive change and healing. The methods which we will consider can be very effective but there is *no guarantee on any approach*. In fact, beware of those programs which claim success if you just follow their guidelines and suggestions to the letter! This creates a sense of guilt and failure if the outcome is not attained. Let's consider some basic problems and then suggest some solutions.

Today we encounter a multitude of family problems, one of which is the breakup of marriages. Many marriages are breakups waiting to happen. They move toward dissolution for years without either person realizing the direction they are going. I see this so often as I talk with couples. For twenty years I have worked with couples attending seminary. Many of them are heading for trouble. All too often the student feels his "spiritual" seminary education must come first and puts his marriage on the shelf until seminary is finished. But more and more frequently it is the marriage that is finished! Marriages die when neglected.

Affairs which occur are not accidents. There are specific reasons for extramarital affairs which can be identified in advance of the affair. Many occur because a partner does not have his or her intimacy needs met in the marriage. Some affairs happen because of the failure to resolve resentments. Drifting in a marriage is a prelude for an affair. This is the feeling that you are going nowhere in the marriage. Little effort is extended, and the rewards are lacking. And the list goes on. But regardless of the reason, when an affair occurs, there is shock, hurt, and a crisis. Perhaps if a controlled, positive crisis were employed earlier, there would be a positive marriage relationship and no affair!

When a spouse learns of an affair, it is like being hit by a tidal wave. But the wave doesn't recede back into the ocean. No matter what else is happening in the person's life, this takes precedence. All other aspects of life come to a halt. There is panic! There is also a tendency to react in such a way that the problem is compounded. The feelings of rejection prompt the typical responses of any grief experience. Some people weep, plead, beg, or make a multitude of promises to bring the person back. And when this doesn't work, the anger begins and can even lead to making threats. In time, a form of acceptance may occur but then the cycle reappears.

I realize I have described a very serious situation which may not apply to you, but remember, many who are married feel the rejection of their spouse for reasons other than an affair. This can include indifference and insensitivity as well as overcontrol.

When any experience of rejection occurs, a typical reaction is panic. And panic leads to appeasement. Responding with appeasement is usually doomed to failure in trying to control the behavior of another person. Parents often use this with their children. You just cannot "buy off" another person. Appeasement often involves a pleading, defenseless response. In time this reinforces the other person's behavior and the person moves further away. Appeasement is not the same as the biblical concept of submission—the voluntary act of putting yourself under the authority of another individual.

A Common Marital Pattern

In my years of counseling I have discovered that marital and family conflict usually involves one person who has invested much more in the relationship than has the other. This person cares more and often is more secure and independent. I have seen many like this and unfortunately the one to whom this person is married never really counted the cost of being married. In fact, I have met a number who should never have married in the first place! But now that they are, the issue is how to help them become a fully functioning, contributing member of the relationship.

When the relationship begins to go downhill, the vulnerable person (the one who has invested the most) is apt to panic. Panicking just conveys the message to the other(s) that you are now out of control and entering your own state of crisis. Now the responses will include begging, pleading, grabbing, crying, becoming angry, or retreating into apathy, passivity, or appeasement.

These are normal reactions but they are rarely successful. In fact, expect them to be counterproductive. The panic reactions can short circuit whatever is left in the relationship. It is a form of confinement which tends to smother the other distant or wayward individual and the person moves further away in order to breathe.

Resistance to Change

When you ask a person to change some behavior that you do not like, he or she will interpret the proposed change in one of four ways:

1) as a *destructive* change;
2) as a *threatening* change;
3) as having *no effect* upon him or her; or
4) as a change that would *help* him or her become a better person. Thus it is important in requesting a change to present the suggestion (if at all possible) in such a way that your spouse sees it as an opportunity for growth.

First of all, expect some resistance. This is normal. If you anticipate this and are aware of the typical forms of resistance, you will be able to handle it much better. Let's consider some typical responses to the request for change and reasons for resistance.

Some people simply stop listening as an expression of their unwillingness to change. They cut off the conversation, leave the room, or busy themselves with some task. A man may stay at the office or a woman may say she has to leave early for an appointment in order to prevent further discussion. This is a form of *withdrawal*.

On the other hand, some people agree with the request, but *they do not follow through on it* because they have no intention of changing. This is a stall tactic to get the person making the request to back off! But after numerous requests with no follow-through, the spouse becomes suspicious and angry.

Or perhaps the person counters with, "Why don't *you* change?" a resistance tactic which *throws the request back to the person making it.* This completely turns the request around and the result will probably be an argument.

Why are we so reluctant to change?

One simple reason for not changing is habit. Day in and day out we maintain a fairly predictable routine. Inside us we have a selection of comfortable responses which make us feel secure. We don't have to think about or work at new ways of responding. But the habits that make us feel secure may be an irritant to others. Habit is probably the most frequently used reason for resistance. Why? Because it works so well.

Have you ever used these excuses or heard them used? "I've always done it this way." "After twenty-eight years, it's too late to change now." "Why change? I'm comfortable. This way works." "How do I know the new way is better? I don't have to think about this one. I just do it."

Perhaps you live with someone who is messy. The person does not: pick up after himself; put items away; hang up his clothes when he comes home from work; change into old clothes before he does a messy chore; pick up the paper and magazines he dropped on the floor; clear his own dishes away from the table.

You may have tried to correct your spouse by begging, pleading, threatening, letting the mess accumulate for days or even weeks, but nothing has worked. Probably your mate was accustomed to having people pick up after him while he was growing up. If this is the case, perhaps he developed the belief that he is special and deserves to be waited on. If he was waited on and picked up after for many years and now his spouse is saying, "Pick up after yourself," the message he is receiving is, "You no longer deserve to be catered to." *Thus his self-esteem is under attack.* The way he thinks about himself has been challenged. This is the real reason why he resists. If he changes he will have to *change some perceptions* he holds about himself. And we don't like to admit that we have been wrong all these years.

But habits can be changed. A habit of twenty-five years can change as quickly as one of ten years or one year once the course of resistance is discovered. The change is easier than most people realize.

There are others who plead ignorance as their resistance. "I didn't think that's what you wanted"; "I don't know how to do that. Who do you think you married? Superman?" Ignorance can be an effective tool because it puts the person making the request on the defensive. She begins to question whether she *did* tell her mate what she wanted or whether she is expecting too much.

Control is another form of resistance that is frequently used. If someone asks me to change I may not comply because of my fear of losing control. I want to stay in control of me and you. The resistance to change comes about because of what that change would communicate about who is in control of the situation. We don't like others determining how we are to behave. The request may not be a control issue but we interpret it in that manner. Anger is often used at this point.

Uncertainty or anxiety are honest resistance responses.

127

"How will this change affect me?" "Will I be capable?" "Will people still respond to me in the same way?" "What if I can't do it to please you?" We anticipate some threats and fears coming into play. *We feel our self-esteem being challenged and threatened, and this again is the key. Any perceived threat to our self-esteem is going to be resisted. "Will I still receive affirmation?" "Will I be as secure?"*

Do you think all your requests for change should meet with instant applause and compliance? If your partner resists your request for change do you become angry, despondent, perplexed, stubborn? Can you see value in resistance? Probably not. But consider the possibilities.

If your requests are resisted, rethink what you are asking. Ask yourself these questions:

1. Why do I want the change?
2. How intensely do I want it?
3. How committed am I to pursuing the change?
4. What does my commitment level to this change tell me about my own needs at this time?

Perhaps the resistance will assist you in being more specific concerning what it is you wish changed. Have you considered your mate's resistance as a unique form of communication? He could be telling you something new about himself—what he values, what elements are involved in his self-esteem. If the person's resistance is too strong, you may need to try another approach.

Change will usually occur if *you* do the following:

1. Examine and clarify your reasons and desires for change. Examine your need.

2. Evaluate your request in light of Scripture. Is this a change which Scripture calls us to make?

3. Understand how the other person sees him/herself and what his/her self-esteem is built upon.

4. Present change in a way that enhances his/her self-esteem.

5. Consider your own willingness to change. Are you willing to stand by the person and encourage, edify, and build him/

her up? Are *you* open to change and is that openness obvious to others? A yes answer to these questions is vital. And remember, if the other person changes, you will need to be willing to adapt to these changes.

6. Use the crisis principle when necessary. (More about that in the next chapter.)

7. Reinforce, reinforce, and reinforce! If the individual makes a requested change and you ignore it or take it for granted, he/she will feel violated, let down, and will revert back to his/her previous behavior. We all need feedback and reward for making a change. Then our self-esteem remains intact. Changes are fragile and must be strengthened. When I *experience* affirmation as a person for my new behavior I feel like making it part and parcel of my lifestyle. If I feel uncertain with this new behavior, then I will return to the certainty of the old. And the new experience and reinforcement needs to be strong. Otherwise, I remember my old experience which is a natural part of my life and is not easily overcome. The reinforcement must come at a time when it can be linked to the new behavior. This means right after it occurs.

8. Be persistent and patient. Don't expect too much too soon and don't become a defeatist.

In the next chapter we will consider some specific ways to bring about change in both major and minor concerns.

11

How to Create a Positive, Constructive Crisis

$\triangledown$

John sat in my office and smiled at me and his wife. The first time I saw him though, he wasn't smiling. He was frustrated and angry. His wife had created a crisis which he didn't know how to handle. He said, "You know, I'm amazed at what has happened in our marriage. In fact," he chuckled, "I'm surprised at how much I've changed. Six months ago, I never thought I would or could change. Nor did I want to. But Trudy's new approach totally confused me and threw me off balance. She approached me differently, talked in a new way and didn't back down when I got upset like she has for years. After a while I realized how serious she was and had to listen. I couldn't predict her anymore. She kept me off balance. I couldn't say this before since I was really angry at first, but I'm glad she did what she did. Boy, I still hate to admit it, but what I was doing was wrong."

What I am going to suggest in this section of the book may surprise, shock, startle, and even offend some readers. That is all right. It is intended to cause you to think—to consider the fact that very possibly you have already inadvertently helped to cause a crisis in someone else's life. I want you to understand that it is possible to precipitate a crisis and bring about change in another person. In fact, there are times when the most loving approach to take with a loved one is to help create a constructive crisis! There are numerous examples of how this has been taking place for many years. Perhaps you are not aware of these planned approaches to creating a crisis.

The desire to see change occur in another person, whether it be a spouse or a child, is very normal. Desiring this change in another person does *not* always reflect a critical attitude on our part. Rather it is an act of caring. But isn't it wrong to try to change others? Isn't it unethical or selfish to expect another person to change his actions or attitude? Often we adopt a hands-off philosophy and assume a pious spirituality! "I will accept my husband (or wife) exactly as he is and not make any attempt to change him." But then if I ask, "Would you like your relationship improved in any way?" the answer is usually "Oh, yes, of course I would."

To improve a relationship means that change must take place in the people involved. Often people say that they can't change another person because people do not change. That is false. People *do* change. We are changing all the time. I have often heard it said, "Well, I'll leave it up to God to change him or her," or "Time is the only factor that will bring about change." Both responses have elements of truth but we *do* have and *can* have significant impact upon others.

How do you feel about the idea of creating a crisis in another person's life? Probably you have some mixed reactions. But consider these facts:

1. We all have the potential for bringing about a crisis in another person's life.

2. There are occasions in all of our lives when we would like to see another person change. (If we're honest, that is.)

3. By not taking direct action in some situations, we allow other individuals to precipitate a crisis in our own life.

4. One of the most loving steps for you, the other person, and the relationship may be to bring about a controlled, con-

structive crisis so that change and growth can occur.

5. Creating the conditions for a crisis to bring about change is much better than engaging in angry tirades, pleading, cajoling, overgiving, nagging, pulling the silent treatment, begging, groveling, pulling your hair, giving up, walking out, involvement in some type of an affair, becoming depressed, or turning your back on God because He doesn't answer your prayers in the matter you want changed!

6. Helping to create a crisis can be a biblically based response because of the desired outcome and the motivation prompting this response.

There are numerous illustrations of a crisis producing change in a person's life. Let's look first of all at the problem of alcoholism and how the crisis approach has become such an effective method of treatment with alcoholism. Alcoholism is a major fatal disease for many people. For years, we have heard that it is only when the alcoholic hits rock bottom and goes through the deepest problems that he or she may be willing to change. Former treatment approaches have not had very positive results.

At the Johnson Institute in Minneapolis, Minnesota, an intervention approach has been developed which has become very successful. Workers at this center were concerned about several questions: Why do people who have the disease wait so long to get help? Why do they suffer so long? Since this disease is so often fatal it is imperative that its progress be stopped as soon as possible. One of the Institute's initial studies of recovered alcoholics revealed that the reason the alcoholics had sought treatment was because a build-up of crises had occurred in their lives. This build-up had forced them into a recognition of their condition. These alcoholic men and women were fortunate because the crises they created and experienced in their family, work, and social relationships were so grouped together that they were able to break through the almost impenetrable defenses which are characteristic of this problem. Alcoholic behavior disrupts the lives of those closely associated with the person and often keeps the others off balance by their irresponsibility and undependability. This and other studies indicate that one does not have to wait until the alcoholic hits bottom. In fact, it is dangerous to do so.

Out of this experience counselors at the Institute have developed a system of treatment based upon creating a crisis. For the alcoholic, the crises are already there so it is not really necessary to create new ones. It is a matter of making the person aware of the crises and using them constructively. Alcoholics are not usually confronted by their own actions and live with an increasing impairment of judgment. It is up to other people to bring this to their attention.

You may be thinking. How does this all apply to me? I don't live with a person who is alcoholic. Perhaps not, but you may be living with a person whose behavior or personality is similar to that of an alcoholic, or with someone who has another type of problem which is becoming unbearable. The principles we will discuss in this chapter have wide application potential.

The use of crisis and making the alcoholic aware of the crisis of his life is called an intervention. Significant people in the person's life meet with him and gently and specifically confront him with the specific behaviors which are a result of his drinking. The belief at the Johnson Institute is that the alcoholic or chemically dependent person can accept the reality of these statements if they are presented to him in a receivable form. Here are the guidelines to be used in such an intervention. As you read them, consider the possibility of how these could be used in other types of problem areas in a person's life.

Guidelines for Crisis Intervention

1. Meaningful individuals must be the ones to present the facts to the alcoholic. These are people who have an influence upon the person such as family, close friends, employer, employees, and so on. Otherwise the person will easily be able to deny the observations of others. The intervention works best when there is a group of two to three or more because of the support they give to one another.

2. The information given should be specific and describe

events which have already occurred or conditions which exist: "I was there when you yelled at John and his client and it was obvious that you had been drinking." First-hand evidence is the best. Statements that include opinions or generalizations should be avoided.

3. The tone of this confrontation should not be judgmental. This is vital. When an individual is attempting to suggest change in others, it is often defeated by a judgmental tone of voice. Simply state the facts to demonstrate the legitimacy of the concern you are expressing: "I am worried about what is happening to you and this concern is based upon these facts."

4. The main evidence should be tied in directly to the problem which in this case is drinking: "After your dinner last week, I saw you staggering when you left and thought someone else would drive you home. But you drove at excessive speeds with three people in your car."

5. The evidence of the person's behavior needs to be given in some detail and quite explicitly. The alcoholic needs to be given a panoramic view of himself over a given period of time: "You spilled your dinner plate and when you walked you bumped into three people." This helps the individual face the reality of his behavior. The alcoholic does not remember these events and must be confronted with them. Some concerned individuals go so far as to make video or audio tapes of the person's behavior to validate what they are saying.

6. The goal of this intervention is to have the person see and accept enough reality so that he will accept his need for help.

7. The final step is to offer to the individual several available choices for assistance. Perhaps the key person is the one to offer the choices. In the case of an alcoholic it might be a treatment center or hospital. Give the alcoholic some choice in the decision-making process. But realize that he may have many excuses for his behavior. Continue to urge the person to make a choice about his treatment. Let's go back now and simplify the various steps up to this point:

1. Significant individuals present the facts to the person.

2. Describe specific events which have already occurred.
3. Do not be judgmental but present the facts.
4. Tie in the evidence to the main problem.
5. Give the evidence in detail and explicitly.
6. The goal is to present reality so the person is willing to seek help.
7. Offer the person several choices for treatment.

What can you learn from this approach to apply to other situations? How would this approach work with a child or adolescent who is becoming unmanageable? How would this work with a spouse who acts as though the marriage isn't of value? How could it work with a spouse who mistreats his or her partner physically? How could this apply to a person who does not seem interested in investing the time necessary to build a close, intimate marriage? Would this be effective with an unfaithful spouse?

Tough Love

Let's consider now a program which was developed to deal with adolescents. It is called Tough Love and was designed to help parents whose teenagers were engaging in some form of destructive behavior. Some of these behaviors are the following:

> Living in filthy bedrooms and saying that it is their room and they can do what they want.
>
> Leaving dirty dishes around and claiming that they did not do it.
>
> Fighting with siblings and saying that their brothers and sisters started it.
>
> Fighting with their parents and saying that Mom or Dad was nagging them.
>
> Consistently coming home late and saying they forgot the time, ran out of gas, their watch was slow, and so on.
>
> Stealing objects from their homes and denying it.
>
> Stealing money from parents, grandparents, brothers, and sisters and denying it.

135

Bringing home rude, unkempt people and blaming the family for making their friends feel uncomfortable.

Playing their stereos at all hours and at ear-shattering levels and claiming they were only listening to music.

Frequently coming home drunk or stoned and saying they were just partying.

Breaking doors, walls, and furniture and claiming they just got angry and could not control themselves.

Avoiding other family members and claiming that their family does not understand them.

Lying around the house all day and staying out all night and saying that they cannot find a job.

Concerning school issues they are:

Getting suspended because teachers are hassling them.

Playing hooky because school is boring and they want to get a job.

Fighting with teachers because they accuse them falsely.

Failing because teachers have it in for them, school is boring, and they have a learning disability.

Not bringing home their report card because they forgot it, lost it, owe money to the library.

Concerning employment issues they are:

Getting fired because the boss was hassling them.

Quitting jobs because they are boring.

Not having money for bills because they did not get paid, lost the money, owed the money to others.

Not getting jobs or job interviews because they forgot, over-slept, had the wrong time, could not find the place, did not have carfare.

Concerning legal issues they are:

Getting fined for disorderly conduct even though the other people started it.

Getting tickets for driving offenses because the policeman did not like them.

Having accidents which were caused by other drivers.

Being accused of robbery even though they were just standing there watching.

Being accused of dealing dope when they were just holding it for someone else.

Shoplifting because the stores charge too much.[1]

This program is for parents who are bothered by unacceptable "adolescent" behavior. It is not limited to parents of teenagers for there are many young adults in their twenties and thirties who are creating the same type of chaos for their parents.

An essential of this program is the parent community support group. This group brings together the parents of these adolescents to help them learn to look at their problems differently. As a result, gradually, they are able to change their responses to their child's behavior and begin to confront their son's or daughter's behavior. They do not try to figure out the child's motivation or the psychological reasons for what is occurring. Instead, they take a close and clear look at their intolerable child's behavior.

It is difficult to do this alone and that is why the support group is vital. The support comes from those who understand and empathize and who do not come in with magical solutions or as superior authority. The support process is quite simple and can include a telephone call or just getting together for a few minutes. The group can help the parents enlist their own families in the process of helping their child instead of hiding the problem from them.

There are ten major beliefs in the Tough Love program and one of them is *taking a stand.* The family with the support of others must stop the child's destructive behavior by taking a stand, thus causing a crisis in the young person's life. This is sometimes difficult for the parents to do because they find it scary and new. But this is what makes the program work! One of the first steps is for the parents to do a crisis assessment. Here is a sample one which is just an illustration and must be adapted for the particular problem. A mother was asked to complete this assessment concerning her daughter:

How often has your teenager come home:
( ) missing dinner
( ) high
( ) late

How often has your teenager run away:
( ) overnight
( ) two days
( ) a week

How often has your teenager been violent:
( ) verbally
( ) physically to the house or furniture
( ) physically to you or your spouse

How often have you or your spouse lost time from work because of your teenager?

How often have you not had a peaceful night's sleep?

How many times has your teenager been late for school?

How many fines has your teenager received?

How many drinking incidents has your teenager been charged with? [2]

As the parents record their responses they can determine whether the number of incidents is increasing or decreasing. This often shows that the parents may be denying the amount of bad behavior because of the pain it causes them.

Most of the people who seek out the Tough Love groups have much in common. They feel in crisis over what is happening in their family and the usual methods of responding (such as reasoning, scolding, punishing, and counseling) have not worked. It may have lifted the problem for a brief period of time, and then the destructive behavior resumes. The parents begin to accept the undesirable behavior as it increases without realizing that it is increasing in intensity. They essentially deny what is taking place.

The Tough Love group approach can help parents stop

denying the problem. They are asked to be as specific as possible about behaviors they don't like and their frequency of occurrence. By sharing this information with the other group members, they are able to become realistic about what is happening in their family and what is bothering them about their child. This helps the parents come to the place where they are willing to take a stand. What does taking a stand actually do? It takes away the adolescent's ability to generate a crisis for others and puts that power into the hands of the parents. This power, if used creatively and with the support of a Tough Love group, can become a very productive tool. Taking a stand means no longer tolerating the irresponsible behavior and allowing the young person to experience the consequences of his or her behavior. The Tough Love approach helps parents stop the crisis which keeps them helpless and puts the consequences of the negative behavior back on the person who is responsible. *Tough Love recommends that parents give their adolescents the crisis instead of hanging onto it.*

After parents have decided to take a stand, the stage is set for a crisis to occur. This could involve stating, as one set of parents did, "We will not accept criminal behavior or cover for you anymore." This means the young person has to avoid breaking the law or accept the consequences. Another set of parents decided they would no longer allow their eighteen-year-old to come home drunk each week. The consequences were such that this young person had to become more responsible for what he was doing.

When parents decide to take a stand they are encouraged to set a "bottom line" which helps move them toward implementing their stand. One set of parents was very concerned about their eighteen-year-old's bouts of drunkenness.

> The family agreed that they would take action after five more binges. That was their bottom line: five more and then action. Perhaps it seems like a weak approach but that's what the parents could tolerate and other group members said they

would be willing to support them. It's better to make a bottom line that people can actually handle than to force a bottom line that's too tough for them to keep. After all, the agreement only lasts a week and people can get progressively tougher as they gain strength from their own changed behavior and their growing trust in the Tough Love's group support.

Further defining the bottom line and the support they would receive from their group, the parents decided that after their son came home drunk a fifth time they would refuse to permit him to stay in their home until he had a drug and alcohol evaluation and agreed to follow the evaluator's recommendations. A group member who lived on the next block agreed that she would call every day to see how things were going and that she would be available to take their son to the evaluation while another family agreed to provide a place for him to stay if necessary.

Five days after the meeting the young man had accomplished his fifth drunk. The parents were both furious and terrified: furious that he hadn't stayed sober even one day, terrified about insisting that he have a drug and alcohol evaluation, a confrontation which might (at least in their fears) drive him away to become a derelict.

The support person was on her way over when she met the young man carrying a duffle bag. He reported that he was going to live at a friend's house and he didn't want or need her help. He wasn't heard from for four days.

What a frightening and trying time for the parents. They were overwhelmed with doubt, fear, and anger. As people do during such anxious periods, the parents also became very blaming. Blaming themselves for taking drastic action, blaming the Tough Love group for encouraging them to do so, blaming anyone and everyone.

The group members understood the anxiety, many having had similar experiences. They called, came over, checked with the boy's friends, the police, and hospitals, but mostly encouraged the parents to persist. They had taken a stand and precipitated a crisis. They were now in a position to control that crisis and create positive change, but the next move was up to their son.

On the fourth day they received a collect call from their

son in Los Angeles. (They lived in New Jersey.) Their son informed them that he had hitchhiked to the West Coast and tried to find a job. There was no work available, said he, and he wanted money to come home. His mom got his telephone number and said that she would call him back shortly.

Mom called her support people for advice. At first she was encouraged to tell him to hitchhike home, since that's the way he got there, but that was more than she and her husband could bear. So they settled on sending him a one-way, nonrefundable (a wise precaution) bus ticket.

When the bus arrived in Trenton at two in the morning, four Tough Love parents plus his own were at the station to meet him. They all went to another family's home and worked out a temporary arrangement under which he could return home. The plan included: absolutely no drinking, finishing his last semester of high school, working for one of the Tough Love members to earn enough to pay his parents for the bus ticket, and weekly reporting to another Tough Love Dad on how he was doing with his commitments.

We caution readers to realize that the family did not ride off into the sunset, happily ever after. There were still problems, as there are in all families. But the drunkenness and its extremely harmful effect on the normal ebb and flow of family life ended.[3]

Other stands parents might take could include: "I will not allow my teenager to physically abuse me or anyone else in the home," or "I will not allow my daughter to date an older man," or "I will not live with a teenager who is using drugs."

But to sort through feelings and take a stand with a bottom line, it is crucial to have the support of other parents. Risky? Yes, but with a potential positive outcome. Let's consider these steps in other family situations.

12

Requests, Positive Shocks, and Constructive Crisis

▽

If you are looking for a guarantee, *don't* read on. If you are willing to think, become creative, and take a risk, *do* read on.

To help a person change you must *avoid* what I call the "deadly four" responses. It's easy to fall into the trap of using them but they spell defeat. The first two responses are passive.

Resignation: "I give up. I just have to accept the fact that he is always going to leave his clothes all over the house. I haven't found any way to change his sloppy habits and now other people are telling me I just need to accept him as he is. I'm going to have to learn to live with the fact that I'll always have to pick up after my husband."

The acceptance which this woman is exhibiting comes from a feeling of impotence. "I'm stuck and I better learn to live with it." When you resign yourself to accepting another person's undesirable behavior you admit that you are powerless. Soon this begins to erode your sense of self-esteem. And when you start thinking less of yourself, how do you think that affects your view of the other person? You begin to think less of him or her also. You begin to care less for that individual and you may begin to withdraw.

A wife told me, "I've waited too long. John and I are not divorced but we're not really married either. We live in the same house but we're like two single people. We share the same space. We're more apart now. I just know that I've lost all chance I've had to change him. I'm stuck now for life!" Resignation is destructive in a relationship. Soon you will begin to feel a sense of loss for what the relationship could have been. There is a better way to respond.

Martyrdom: A martyr accepts the behavior of others that he feels he is unable to change. But he uses this acceptance to show others how good *he* is. He frequently reminds his mate or child of the sacrifice he is making in putting up with this behavior. This becomes a sore spot in the relationship and the other person learns to tune the martyr out. The martyr in turn withdraws and in time begins to question whether the relationship is actually worth the effort.

There are two rather active, but also deadly, responses to our inability to change another person.

Revenge: "Vengeance is mine," is expressed in small, insignificant ways which may go unnoticed at first. A person who is tightly controlled and dominated by another may begin to lie about his/her activities. For example, a spouse who is restricted financially by the frugality of the other partner may use some of the budgeted money secretly for his or her own use. Other responses are more than obvious and quite direct. Revenge stems from our anger over not being able to change the relationship. But revenge is counterproductive. Does it bring about the change we desire? Not likely. Expressions of revenge may bring about the very same response in the other person.

Withdrawal: This is a declaration that "If I can't change you, then I choose not to be involved with you at all!" In marriage there are degrees of withdrawal ranging from the extreme of divorce or separation to living together as "married singles" sharing only the same house. As one wife explained, "I didn't believe that you could change others but I really wanted

John to change. I tried to accept what he did and said. I had these emotional needs which were never met. But now it doesn't matter. Tomorrow is the third anniversary of our divorce." Caring, love, and commitment become foreigners in a land of pretense for the sake of others. Withdrawal is a costly option.

Make Positive Requests

To constructively help a person change, you must have some kind of a plan in mind. I don't know the situation you are interested in changing. You will first of all have to decide if you can become comfortable with these approaches and then pray, think, and plan how to apply them to your area of concern.

The first thing you need to do is to make a request. You may feel that "I've tried all this before," but have you really? Too often requests are stated or come across as demands. The intensity and tone of voice may carry the real message that you're feeling.

When you make a request, make it specific and positive, not negative and general. Going to your partner and saying, "You're so inconsiderate," or "You're never affectionate," does little to promote change. But saying, "I would really appreciate it if, when you come home, you would come up to me, put your arm around me, and ask how my day was," or "It really makes my day when you put your things away when you come home." Point to the desired behavior rather than pointing out what's lacking. It also conveys the belief that the other person is capable of changing.

Within a Request—Do the Following

First of all, *you must give the person information.* Each person has a different need for and capacity for handling information. For most individuals, the more information you provide about a desired change the less the resistance. Why? Because there is more opportunity for him to see the request for change as a step toward growth. "John, I appreciate your interest in the children and their education. I'd like you to help me in two areas with them—David needs your assistance with some of his projects and I need your help in talking to his teacher. I understand that this may take some time, but your opinions and knowledge can help David more than I can. If we both talk to the teacher we'll be able to share our ideas and also present a united front to both the teacher and David." A person needs to know what you expect of him, why you expect it, and what may be the results.

Involving your partner in exploring various alternatives for change will also lessen resistance. Your spouse will be less defensive if she has a chance to express her ideas and make suggestions. "Jan, you know that we've been able to talk a bit more lately about how the home is kept and also our scheduling difficulties. I'm wondering if we could explore some possible alternatives that might work. This doesn't mean we're going to just accept whatever idea is shared, but just that we get some more ideas to work with. What do you think?"

Start out slowly so that the request is easier to respond to. Is the change requested an overwhelming and gigantic step? Or have you broken the request down into small increments which can actually be accomplished? If so, there may be a better response. If the requested change is for increased communication, starting out sharing for fifteen minutes one night a week is reasonable. Your goal may be thirty minutes a night, four nights a week, but that is too much to expect at first. Having the garage cleaned and kept clean is a typical request. But developing a specific small step plan to accomplish this over a four-month period of time may be workable. Show that you believe the other person is capable of changing.

Intimacy is a final factor. Resistance is a normal response when one partner mistrusts and fears the other. If motives or intentions are questioned, how can a suggested change be seen as anything but damaging? If trust and intimacy exist, a spouse may see the request as one way to achieve even greater intimacy in the marriage. For example, a wife who has responded favorably to her husband's previous suggestions for change will be open if:

1. Her husband acknowledges her change in a positive way.

145

He doesn't say, "Well, it won't last," or "It's about time," or "I can't believe it."

2. He doesn't mention her change or lack of change in front of others to embarrass her.

3. He is open to change himself.

4. She knows he loves her whether she changes or not.

5. She sees his request for change as something that will enhance her life.

A request invites a person to change but doesn't demand it. The relationship will continue regardless of the response and you will still respond to the other person. Requests involve simplicity of speech and honesty. You are responding to what the other person *does* rather than to him as a person. You comment not on what you feel, or think, or infer, but on what you have actually heard or seen. Feedback should be focused on information and alternatives. The more possibilities available, the less hemmed in the person feels. And if they have a contribution to make to the alternatives, they are less resistant.

Do the Unexpected

One of the most basic principles of bringing about change in another person whether it be a spouse, child, employee, or friend, is to *do the unexpected.* Break out of being predictable! This is best done by fragmenting your usual patterns of behavior. Too often in marriage one person begins to act like a machine who is there to meet the needs of the other person forever while denying his own need. Too often we are so predictable. But if you disrupt the routine you are back in control and you will certainly get your spouse's attention!

Let's look at a serious and all-too-common situation. In marriage, when one individual is *leaning out* of the marriage and *even involved* with another person, the usual inclination is to attempt to reach out and bring the person back using whatever means are available. But the type of behaviors usually employed which we have already discussed are predictable and have no positive effect. What then is the answer? Give the other person his freedom! Let him out of his self-imposed and imagined cage. Dr. James Dobson shares the letter of a woman who did just that:

> John, I've been through some very tough moments since you decided to leave, as you know. My love for you is so profound that I just couldn't face the possibility of life without you. To a person like me who expected to marry only once and to remain committed for life, it is a severe shock to see our relationship begin to unravel. Nevertheless, I have done some intense soul searching, and I realize that I have been attempting to hold you against your will. That simply can't be done. As I reflect on our courtship and early years together, I'm reminded that you married me of your own free choice. I did not blackmail you or twist your arm or offer you a bribe. It was a decision you made without pressure from me. Now you say you want out of the marriage, and obviously, I have to let you go. I'm aware that I can no more force you to stay today than I could have made you marry me in 1972 [or whenever]. You are free to go. If you never call me again, then I will accept your decision. I admit that this entire experience has been painful, but I'm going to make it. The Lord has been with me thus far and He'll go with me in the future. You and I had some wonderful times together, John. You were my first real love and I'll never forget the memories we shared. I will pray for you and trust that God will guide you in the years ahead.[1]

What might happen if the person were given his freedom? Dr. Dobson suggests three possible consequences when the offended partner begins to let go of the resistant spouse.

1. The confined or trapped person no longer feels that it is necessary to fight off the other and the relationship can improve. The strain and tension begin to lift.

2. As the resistant or indifferent partner begins to feel free, the question he or she has been asking for some time may change from, "How can I get out of this?" to "Do I really want to go?" There is a basic principle in this which is such

a reflection of our human nature. When we can have our own way and the other individual no longer fights us but encourages us in that direction, what we wanted so often loses its appeal. Encouraging the other person to do what he or she wants to do shifts the power from that person to you.

I have seen this work time and time again in counseling. A wife complained to me about her husband's discourtesy by not calling her to let her know when he was going to be late. She had nagged him for years but to no avail. I suggested that since this wasn't working, why not encourage him *not* to call when he was going to be late. She could say, "Honey, I know that often things come up at the office and you're later than you intended. That's fine. I understand. Don't worry about calling to let me know. I can adjust quite well. I can keep your dinner in the oven, and if you're not hungry, I can save it for the next day if you want it. And if I need to go out, I'll leave you a note." Amazing, that after two weeks of this, the husband began to call home to let her know when he was going to be late. If two people do not want to give up their manner of quarreling and fighting, encouraging them to continue actually weakens their response and they begin to consider another way of responding.

3. A third change which can occur happens in the mind of the hurt partner. She begins to feel better because she is taking charge of her own life once again and not allowing the other individual to affect her so much. Personal respect begins to return and the feeling of control occurs through letting go. Because there is some sort of a plan to follow, the person experiences more control.[2]

Create a Crisis

Whenever there are behaviors within a marriage or family relationship that are destructive and detrimental, such as infidelity or abuse, one of the best approaches is to create a major crisis. This approach is not going to be easy because it is going to go counter to many years of reinforcing patterns of behavior and response. This is where Dr. Dobson's book title, *Love*

Must Be Tough, is so appropriate. You must be tough but loving. You must take a stand. An individual who is an abuser, an adulterer, an alcoholic, gambler, and so on is helped the most by being confronted with his or her behavior and given a loving ultimatum. The person is *not* helped by being allowed to continue his behavior and having his spouse cover for him.

Before you confront your spouse about a severe marital problem, there are several steps you need to take. First of all, you need prayerfully to consider what to do and spend quantities of time seeking God in prayer. Secondly, it may be helpful to discuss what to do with a qualified person who believes in this approach. Thirdly, spend time writing down the typical ways you respond to your spouse's bad behavior including the specific statements you make. Then write out and rehearse out loud what you are going to say instead. Try to anticipate your spouse's response so you can prepare yourself for his or her reply.

Be sure you are familiar with the use of the broken record technique in case you need to use this. It has proven to be very effective. The broken record technique is simply being persistent and saying over and over again what you want without becoming angry, obnoxious, irritated, loud, or out of control. You stick to your point as though you were a record with the needle stuck. You ignore all side issues which are brought up and also ignore a request for reasons behind the confrontation ("Why are you doing this to me?"). You are not thrown by what the other person says and you continue to be persistent.

Joan: Jim, I'm concerned about the amount of time that you've been gone and I thought it might be helpful for us to look over our schedules.

Jim: Oh, good grief. There you go again, griping about my schedule. You like the money I bring home, don't you?

Joan: I understand you're making good money but I am concerned about the amount of time that you're gone and would like to talk about it.

Jim: Well, my schedule is set and that's that. What about

you? What do you do with all the time you spend around here? The house could use some cleaning.

Joan: You could be right about the house and I will work on it. I am concerned about the amount of time that you're gone and feel it would be good for both of us to look at our schedules.

Jim: Look at what? Why should I be here more? We don't do anything!

Joan: Jim, I am concerned about your time away and would really like to discuss this with you.

Jim: (*pause*) Well, what's there to discuss? Go on.

When you are repetitive and persistent, the other person often realizes that he or she is not going to sidetrack you and perhaps reluctantly begins to discuss the issue.

A secular book whose specific suggestions on this subject and dialog I have found very helpful is *When I Say No I Feel Guilty* by Manuel Smith (Bantam).

An example in a more serious situation might be a statement like, "Jim, I understand that you are interested in seeing another woman. That is your choice but it is creating a major problem in our lives. I want you to hear what I am saying. If you continue to see this person, we will separate. It is your choice and you need to make the decision." Then say no more. The more said, the worse it is. No, separation is not the only approach and it must be used wisely. Above all, you must be willing to follow through with whatever you say you are going to do. This can create a crisis as the person begins to experience the consequences of his or her behavior.

The attitude with which you create this crisis is the main element to consider. A timid, pleading, or hostile, angry approach is not the answer. Becoming angry with a child is not effective nor is it with a spouse. Action is needed. A calm, serious confidence must be expressed. This is why it is important to rehearse and practice what is going to be said in advance. *Do not* share all the pain and hurt which you have experienced. *Do not* share all of what you are thinking or plan to do—and above all don't be predictable! This can include changing your daily routine, the way you fix meals or do tasks around the home, your time table, how much you talk, and so on. Show that you are strong and in control. But you do need to act in love. Don't do anything that might undermine the person's relationship with other members of the family who don't know what is happening. Your goal is to build a new relationship.

Sometime back a woman made an appointment to see me. When she came in it was apparent what at least part of her problem was. One eye was blackened and patches of hair were missing from her head, the result of her husband pounding her head against the bathroom floor. She was terrified by her husband at this point. They had been married for ten years and had two young children. He was fairly well known in the community and was a Sunday school teacher at their church. He was respected by others and had served on the church board at one time. Once a month he exploded with no visible provocation or warning. The beatings had become more frequent and violent and were physically apparent on the victim. Recently, she had experienced bruised ribs which hindered her ability to do the housework. In time, her husband became irate over this which had caused the latest incident.

When the man was willing to discuss the problem, he blamed his wife. Most of the time he refused to talk about the incident and demanded that she do as he said.

As she talked, she cried in frustration. For three years, he had been beating her and no one knew about it. "He's like a Dr. Jekyll and Mr. Hyde," she said to me. "When he's nice, he's nice. But when he's mean, watch out. I shouldn't be here today. He'll flip when he finds out! I'm afraid for the children as well. What should I do? I want my marriage. I do care for him but I can't take the violence any more. I don't believe in divorce but I don't believe in this either. I'm tired of doing his bidding, and it doesn't keep him from becoming angry. So, now what?"

She had several options and the consequences of each needed to be considered carefully.

1. She could continue as she had been doing. Allow the situation to exist. But this would just reinforce the possibility

of being beaten again. Without realizing it, allowing the situation to continue merely encouraged her husband to continue his violence. He was not the one experiencing negative consequences. Being passive will not work.

2. Divorce him. This was not an option for her and thus was not the answer.

3. Emotionally insulate herself. Without realizing it, she may have already started the process which creates an emotional divorce so the psychological can be blocked out. But the physical will continue and emotional insulation carries the risk of deadening yourself emotionally to others or becoming overly vulnerable and open to an affair.

4. Take charge of the situation and create a crisis. This is no guarantee but a risky approach like this has worked for many. Right now she is allowing herself to be both abused and controlled and he is continuing to learn that he can get away with this.

I suggested that she plan in advance a statement that she would like to make to her husband about this situation. It should be simple, factual, and give her intentions. It would help to write it out and verbally rehearse it. It may help to rehearse it with another person. Then, either at a time when her husband is demanding that she do something unreasonable or at a calm moment she should make her statement. This will probably upset him and throw him off balance, but the crisis it precipitates may change the destructive marital pattern. Here are the steps to follow if you find yourself in a similar situation:

>>Let a trusted friend, relative, or counselor know about the problem and what you intend to do. Stay away from those who disagree with this approach or give a lot of unsolicited advice.

>>Arrange for a safe place to stay for yourself and the children if necessary. Make financial plans for this step as well.

>>Be committed to follow through once this procedure is started.

>>Make a statement to your spouse along these lines:

I have something I need to share with you and I want you to hear me out. Because I care about you, myself, and our marriage, I am going to make some changes. First of all, I will no longer be doing everything that you demand of me. We will discuss the issues as two adults. You may become upset at this but that is your choice.

Secondly, I will no longer submit to nor tolerate any physical violence on your part. If you ever lay a hand on me again, I will take two steps. I will call the authorities and press charges and I will separate from you and take the children with me. And because I care about you, myself, and the children, we will stay separated until you have begun professional help for yourself and we both enter into marriage counseling.

Thirdly, I feel that in order to overcome what causes you to respond with such anger and violence, I want you to seek professional help at this time. I have discussed this concern with others and they agree with me. I have the name of a professional counselor and I am willing to go with you if you so desire. And I will continue to make this latter request of you each week until you go for help.

>>When you know the time you are going to share this with your spouse, ask those who are aware of the problem to be praying for you.

>>Your statement should be presented calmly, slowly, and with confidence. But, what happens if he interrupts, goes into a rage, stalks out, or becomes violent?

If he interrupts, lean forward or stand up, and use hand motions to indicate that you are interrupting him and say, "Please wait until I've finished" in a calm, directive voice. Then start over.

If he raises objections, argues, becomes angry, use the broken record approach and repeat word for word what you said. If he starts to become violent, take the children and leave. Put your statement into action. There are some other alternatives to use with this approach as well.

If your spouse tends to excessive violence, enlist the support of a minister or family members to be there when you make your confrontation. You are the spokesman and they are there for physical support and protection.

If your church has a couple where a spouse is a now reformed abuser, enlist their support for the confrontation.

Either write out your statement word for word or make a cassette tape and send it to your husband at work via certified mail. Indicate that you will meet him at a specific time for dinner at a quiet restaurant to discuss the situation. Get a babysitter to take care of the children for the evening.

These are all unexpected, unpredictable, different behaviors indicating that you mean business. They may sound like radical suggestions, but destructive behavior calls for radical changes. No one can guarantee the outcome but if some new approach isn't employed, either the marriage or a life will be destroyed!

I've heard of even more extreme measures. One wife who was physically abused took matters into her own hands. She waited until her husband was asleep next to her and then pulled back the covers and poured ice water on his stomach. Naturally, he awoke with a start and began an angry tirade. She interrupted him, pointed a finger in his face, and calmly and softly said, "This time it was ice water. If you ever hit or slap me again, the next time it will be battery acid. Good night, dear." And she went to bed! Now, I'm not suggesting this but you do have to admit, it got his attention. And he never struck her again.

Let me throw out a suggestion which has not yet been fully worked through and needs refinement. It is a recommendation for the church to consider. Remember the approach of the family confrontation that is used for the alcoholic? I wonder what would happen, in the case of a person who is breaking the marriage vows, abusing a family member, or involved in some other activity which threatens the family, if a select group from the church who are aware of the problem would make a similar type of confrontation? This could include family members, church officials, friends, and so on. Along this line I would encourage you to read the book, *Healing the Wounded—The Costly Love of Church Discipline* by John White and Ken Blue (Intervarsity Press). (See especially chapter 10.)

What I am suggesting involves a risk! There is no guarantee as to the outcome. Consistent firmness, love, sensitivity, and tact are needed on your part. Risking and growing is a bit fearful because you are giving up something without knowing for certain if the outcome will be any better. When you change you are giving up an old way of seeing yourself and this may be uncomfortable. Why? Because you are saying that what you have been doing hasn't been the best and the new way is better. We don't really like to be self-critical and discover that we have been ineffective in some way.

Whenever you take a risk there is going to be some unavoidable loss. You have to give up something to move ahead. But not risking is one of the best ways of losing what we desire. And if we don't take the risk and stay in charge of it, the risk will occur anyway and we won't be in charge. It is much better to have something to say about it.

"I am afraid to take this step—this risk," you may say. That is normal and it is best to be open about your fear. You are not sure where you are going to land after you leap. You are concerned about the loss which is implied in every risk and the possible failure of the risk itself. But what about the hurt sustained by not risking? Which is more painful? If you don't take the opportunity to change when the time is right, you will probably have to change when you do not want to and you will be out of control.

Many of the people I meet are in prison. Not a federal penitentiary to which they have been sentenced by a judge in our court system, but a prison of their own making. In our desire for stability and security we shun risks and in so doing create a prison around us. Howard Hughes was one of the wealthiest men alive and yet in his last years he attempted to insulate himself from germs, strangers, decisions, and risk of any kind. He kept to himself for years in his self-imposed cell and lived a terrible life within his own self-imposed solitary confinement.

To summarize what we have discussed about creating a constructive crisis, you will need to:

1. Have a specific goal of what you would like to accomplish. Without a clear purpose, you are in difficulty right from the start.

2. Identify the loss that will be involved. If you don't expect it, your efforts can be undermined.

3. Act decisively. Identify and focus on the factors which can make it work. Don't dwell on all of the problems and "what ifs . . . ." When you pass another car on the highway, you need to act decisively and not hesitate and waver. Indecision can be fatal.

4. Don't ignore the problems. Anticipate them by working toward their solution. Don't use them as an anchor to keep you stuck in the mud.

5. Avoid being unrealistic. Identify the best effort you can make and do not plan on other people or elements you can't control or that are not available.

6. Don't deny or avoid your emotions. A risk should not be taken out of uncontrolled or excessive anger, guilt, depression, and so on. Deal with those feelings on their own.

7. Don't rush into what you are going to do without proper preparation, planning, and prayer. On the other hand, don't procrastinate and "wait for the right time." Often the right time has to be created.

Solving Everyday Problems

Most of the examples and situations described here are major crises. But what about using this approach earlier in order to prevent the occurrence of some of these family difficulties? Can this approach be used in everyday noncrisis adjustment difficulties? Yes, they can!

For the less serious but important concerns, creating a major crisis is not what I'm suggesting. Perhaps it would be better to call it a minor crisis or a positive shock. Whatever it is called, it is designed to get the person's attention. Think how you would feel if you were in the following situation. You enter an elevator with several other people on the first floor for a ride to the twelfth floor. The elevator is just half filled. It stops to pick up a passenger on the second floor and instead of walking in, turning, and facing the door like the rest of you, he stands facing you, not saying a word, scanning your faces. A bit unnerving. You bet it is! It was a bit of a shock.

I can remember a time when my wife used a positive shock experience to help me change. A number of years ago I had the habit of not hanging up my pajamas in the morning when I got up and dressed. I would toss them toward the hook on the door where they belong. Sometimes my basketball shots landed, but most of the time I missed. And from time to time, Joyce suggested to me that it might be nice if I would hang them up myself each day. But nothing seemed to change.

I will never forget the day I was sitting on the couch reading the paper when Joyce came up and sat next to me with my pajamas folded neatly on her lap. She put her arm around me, smiled, and said, "Norm, you are a man of excellent organizational ability and deep concern for being precise, accurate, in control, and orderly. I just know you would delight in knowing that when you left for work each day, you could reflect back and remember that when you arose and started the day, you had taken off your pajamas, walked over to the hook on the closed door, and carefully hung first the tops and then the bottoms on the appropriate hook. I'm sure that would really help make your day. Thank you for listening." And with that she stood up and left the room.

I was taken totally off guard. I had listened a bit shocked at this unusual approach and I sat there grinning. But little did I know what had been done to me because about a month later I realized that since that day I had been hanging up my pajamas! I was hardly aware that I was changing but she certainly got my attention!

Here are some actual life situations in which a positive shock or small crisis was created to bring about change.

Case 1

Joan was becoming more and more frustrated about her husband who was becoming a full-fledged workaholic. He was very conscientious about his work but was rarely home and had not taken any vacation time for three years. Joan was virtually raising the children by herself and her attempts to convey her concern to her husband were met by excuses and promises that if she would just be patient for a few more months, he might be able to cut back. But he was in a job where essentially he controlled his own time.

Having seen the destructive results of this pattern in other families, Joan decided that she had to get his attention. One day at work Tom received a telegram requesting his presence that evening for dinner with "one of his most valuable clients." He was told to be at a restaurant at 7:00 that night which was one of the finest in the city. The telegram stated that it was important for him to be there since he was on the verge of losing this important client. Reservations had been made in his name. He was totally befuddled and perplexed and no one he talked to, from fellow workers and secretaries to restaurant personnel, could shed any light on the situation.

He decided that he would go and he did. When he arrived, he was shown to a table and told that the other party would be a few minutes late. A few minutes later, much to his surprise, his wife Joan walked in, smiled, and sat down. He was stunned.

"Did you send the telegram? Are you the client? What is this?" he asked.

"Yes, I did send the telegram and I am the client," she replied. "I need to talk to you. I feel as though I am one of your neglected clients and because of the past three years, I was wondering when it is that you were planning to drop me out of your life."

Tom was shocked. His next few responses were met with

that same question, "When are you planning to drop me out of your life?"

Finally, he said, "What do you mean? I've never planned to drop you. I care for you. I need you. I love you. I always want you with me."

"I don't feel that you want me or need me," Joan replied. "I love you and want our marriage. But I feel as though I'm a stranger to you. I know your work is important. I appreciate your dedication and diligence but I want your time, diligence, and dedication for our marriage as well. I want to spend this evening with you. So let's go ahead and order dinner and you can continue to think about what I've said.

"If you would like to talk about what we will be doing to build our marriage," she continued, "I will listen. But I will not listen to excuses or reasons for not taking action now. I want action and I want you! Let's eat."

Needless to say, Joan did get his attention. Fortunately, her plan worked. In his discussion with her, he admitted that her radical approach captured his attention and let him know how serious she was.

Case 2

Marie was a twenty-one-year-old college student. Her parents had divorced three years before and she lived with her mother while she attended college. Her father lived a mile away and had never really adjusted to the divorce. He wanted his daughter to spend time with him, but whenever she did she heard nothing but complaints about her mother and her. Her father wanted to know why she didn't spend more time with him, what her mother was saying, and would vent his anger over the divorce. Marie was torn between her love for and her feelings of obligation toward her father, and the resulting upset which she always experienced. Recently Marie put into action her plan of positive shocks to change the relationship and ensuing discussions. As she and her father were sitting in a restaurant eating dinner the conversation turned toward why she didn't spend more time with her dad. While he was talking, Marie interrupted and said, "Dad, I have something I would like you to hear. I love you and I want you to know that. I am comfortable with the amount of time I spend with you and I will not be increasing it. If anything, it may decrease because of the constant pressure I feel when we are together. I have heard many times before what you have said about me, Mom, and the divorce. I understand your feelings but nothing more can be accomplished by you discussing these issues with me. If you persist in bringing them up, I will leave. I would rather do that than become angry and swear at you as I have done before. Please, let's change the subject."

But her father continued to pursue the subject. Marie interrupted again and this time was a bit more definite, repeating essentially what she had said before. When her father continued, she rose from the table and said, "Dad, I'll be leaving now. Please call me when you would like to get together again and we will try another time. 'Bye." And with that she walked out.

Her father was angry and shocked. Later in the week he tried to talk to her about what she had done and how she had embarrassed him. But she refused to discuss it and proceeded on as though it had not occurred. On the next two occasions, the same thing happened and again she left. But after that, her father told her that he now realized that she was serious and asked her (for the first time) what she would like for their relationship and what she would be comfortable in discussing. Her persistence helped not only to salvage the relationship, but also to build a closer one.

Case 3

George and Sally were in their mid-thirties. Their marriage was fairly healthy and would have been better except for George's parents. They were very demanding and often dictated where George and Sally would be for holidays and even for some of their vacations. Sally was becoming more and more upset and George was also at the end of his rope. They began to talk about how to handle his parents in a more effective manner and also how to deal with the manipulation and ensuing guilt feelings which always seemed to occur. They talked with several other couples and read two or three books on assertive approaches. Here is the conversation which was the first positive shock George's parents experienced.

Mom: Hello, George, this is Mom.

George: Hi, Mom, how are you doing?

Mom: Oh, all right I guess. (She sighs.)

George: Well fine, but how come you're sighing?

Mom: Oh, well, I guess I haven't been doing too good. I don't know what's wrong. Anyway, are you coming over this weekend? I was hoping to see you. You know it's been several weeks since you and Sally have been here.

George: I'm sorry you're not feeling too well, Mom. No, we won't be coming over this weekend. We have some other things that we have already planned to do.

Mom: Well, what's more important than seeing your dad and mom? Aren't we important to you anymore?

George: I can understand that you want to see us, Mom, and you are important, but we won't be coming over this weekend.

Mom: Well, we sure are disappointed. We were positive that you would be over, and I already have a turkey for dinner. Did you know that?

George: No, Mom, I didn't.

Mom: Both your father and I are disappointed. Here we were expecting you to come and we have the turkey already bought.

George: Mom, I can tell that you're disappointed, but we won't be able to be there this weekend.

Mom: You know your brother and sister come over to see us all the time. We don't even have to ask them!

George: That's true, Mom. They do come over more and I'm sure they are a lot of company. We can plan for a visit another time and work it out in advance.

Mom: A good Christian son wants to see his parents often.

George: Does my not coming over make me a bad Christian son?

Mom: If you really loved and cared for us, you would want to come and see us.

George: Does my not coming to see you this weekend mean that I don't love you?

Mom: It just seems that if you did, you would be here.

George: Mom, not coming over does not mean I don't care for both of you. I love you and Dad. But I won't be there this time. I'm sure you can use the turkey now or freeze it. Now, let me check with Sally and you look at your schedule and see when we could all get together.

By planning and rehearsing this approach in advance George was able to take a stand with a minimum of guilt feelings. As he and Sally continued this approach they became much more comfortable with their relationship. As George's parents began to back off, George and Sally felt freer to initiate get-togethers they could all enjoy. And his parents began to enjoy the visits more since they were no longer the pursuers.

Case 4

Paula and Rex had been married for ten years. Rex was an engineer and deeply involved with his profession and his church. Their marriage appeared to be quite good from all external appearances. But there was little if any emotional intimacy, mainly because Rex did not know how to share his emotions and avoided expressing his feelings, especially when Paula began, as he called it, one of their "emotional discussions."

Paula was slowly starving to death emotionally and was concerned that the rest of her married life would be emotionally vacant. She pressured Rex, begged him, cried, and became angry but nothing seemed to work. She wanted not only the emotional interaction but some time and attention from Rex. Rex was becoming more and more preoccupied out of his fear of emotional interactions with Paula.

Fortunately, however, Paula began following a new approach. She began showing much more self-confidence and independence, without giving an explanation for what she was doing. Whereas before she depended heavily on Rex and asked his opinion on practically everything in her attempt to engage him in the relationship, she now reversed her approach. She scheduled some activities for herself without consulting him and was no longer the pursuer.

Rex began to share a bit more with her as the pressure on him decreased. One evening as he was talking, Paula said, "You know, I appreciate how clearly and factually you communicate with me. That's helpful to me. You're very good at sharing the facts and the logical prints. In fact, much better than I am. I'm much more into emotions and that's where my skill and strengths lie. I can sure learn a lot from the way you think and communicate. I appreciate that. Some day, when you are ready and interested in learning about emotions and feelings, let me know and I think I have some new information which might amaze you. In fact, it will change a lot of your life, not only with me, but with everyone else with whom you come in contact."

With that she went into the other room and busied herself doing the dishes. She did not mention the subject again for several days. A few days later they were in a discussion and Paula asked Rex how he felt about an issue. She quickly corrected herself and said, "I'm sorry, I didn't mean to ask how you felt about that. I meant what did you think about it?"

"Wait a minute!" Rex replied. "I can handle that question about my feelings! I'm not dead, you know. And by the way, you made a statement about learning about emotions and feelings. What did you mean about that?"

"Do you really want to know?" Paula asked.

"Yes, I do," Rex said.

"Well, I appreciate that," Paula replied. "We need more time than we have tonight. Can I take you out to dinner tomorrow night where we have some privacy and enough time to talk? I have a new place picked out which serves your favorite food. How does that sound?"

Rex hesitated and said, "Well, why not now?"

Paula replied, "Let's talk tomorrow night, okay?" And they did. Rex was puzzled and intrigued by Paula's response. In a sense, he was no longer in control of the situation.

At dinner the next evening, Paula shared her love and commitment for Rex. She also shared her need for emotional intimacy and said, "I understand that I have pressured you and I am sorry for that. We both came into this marriage speaking different languages. You spoke facts, brief sentences, and a lot of logic. I talked more, shared feelings, and used different words. We each spoke a foreign language. I think we can both learn each other's language and have an even better relationship. What do you think?" She kept asking his opinion using his language; finally she suggested, "I have found two books which I think can make a difference. If you would like to read them, I have them for you. But if you are not ready and would like more time to consider our discussion, that would be fine. We don't have to do it now."

"Well, wait a minute," Rex said. "I would like to see what you have." Paula reached into her handbag and pulled out two books. One was *Why Am I Afraid to Tell You Who I Am?* by John Powell (Argus) and the other was *The Secrets Men Keep—Breaking the Silence Barrier* by Dr. Ken Druck and James Simmons (Doubleday). Without comment she gave both to Rex. She did not mention the books again until Rex began to talk about them. In fact, he started reading some of the pages to her. Within weeks their relationship began to change and Rex started to discover the world of feelings and vulnerability. Fortunately, this couple's story had a positive ending. Many do, but there are other couples where either the husband or the wife is so ingrained in a particular way of living life that they may continue to retreat even with this approach. That's the risk but it is better than taking no action at all.

Remember what I said earlier? *Do the unexpected* and *don't be predictable!* Keep track of what you do and what you say for several days and note the other person's response. Next, in writing, describe what you would need to do in order to be unpredictable and different. Then rehearse the new statements and map out in detail how you will use them. Try to anticipate your spouse's responses, both positive and negative. Practice. Practice. Discuss your new approach with a *trusted* friend or counselor. Be sure you ask yourself the question: Am I willing to change as much as I want the other person to change? One of the best ways to help another person to change is to become a pacesetter in change yourself. Philippians 3:12–14 says:

> Not that I have already obtained it, or have already become perfect, but I press on in order that I may lay hold of that for which also I was laid hold of by Christ Jesus. Brethren, I do not regard myself as having laid hold of it yet; but one thing I do: forgetting what lies behind and reaching forward to what lies ahead, I press on toward the goal for the prize of the upward call of God in Christ Jesus.

Notes

Chapter 1

1. H. Norman Wright, *Crisis Counseling* (San Bernardino, Calif.: Here's Life Publishers, 1985), pp. 8–15 (adapted).

2. Lewis B. Smedes, *How Can It Be All Right When Everything Is All Wrong?* (New York: Harper and Row, 1982), pp. 16, 17. Used by permission.

3. Charles R. Swindoll, *Growing Strong in the Seasons of Life* (Portland, Ore.: Multnomah Press, 1983), pp. 274, 275. Used by permission.

Chapter 2

1. Some material in this chapter has been adapted from Lloyd H. Ahlem, *Living with Stress* (Ventura, Calif.: Regal Books, 1978).

2. Adapted from Ann Kaiser Stearns, *Living through Personal Crisis* (New York: Ballantine Books, 1984), pp. 65, 66.

3. Ibid., pp. 71, 72 (adapted).

4. Ibid., pp. 85, 86.

5. Based on a similar chart from Ralph Hirschowitz, in "Addendum," a special feature of the *Levinson Letter* (Cambridge: The Levinson Institute, n.d.), p. 4.

Chapter 3

1. Arthur J. Snider, "Twenty-five Most Distressing Events in Your Life," *Science Digest* (May 1971), pp. 68–72.

2. Clark Blackburn and Norman Lobsenz, *How to Stay Married* (New York: Cowles Books, 1968), p. 196.

3. B. L. Neugarten, "Time, Age, and the Life Cycle," *American Journal of Psychiatry* (1979), pp. 136, 189 (adapted).

4. David C. Morley, *Halfway Up the Mountain* (Old Tappan, N.J.: Fleming H. Revell, 1979), p. 26.

Chapter 4

1. Dr. Herbert J. Freudenberger, *Burnout: How to Beat the High Cost of Success* (New York: Bantam Books, 1980), pp. 17–19.

2. I. David Welch, Donald C. Medeiros, and George A. Tate, *Beyond Burnout* (Englewood Cliffs, N.J.: Prentice-Hall, Inc., 1982), pp. 13, 14.

3. Freudenberger, *Burnout*, p. 206.

Chapter 5

1. Much of this chapter is adapted from Wright, _Crisis Counseling_ (see chap. 1, n. 1).

2. Meyer Friedman and Diane Ulmer, _Treating Type A Behavior and Your Heart_ (New York: Alfred A. Knopf, 1984), pp. 36–43 (adapted).

3. Ibid., p. 62.

4. Ibid., p. 67 (adapted).

5. Lloyd Ogilvie, _God's Best for Today_ (Eugene, Ore.: Harvest House, 1981), February 3.

6. Adapted from Dr. Dwight Carlson.

7. Orin L. Crain.

8. Author unknown.

9. Friedman and Ulmer, _Treating Type A Behavior,_ pp. 166–96 (adapted); also Rosalind Forbes, _Life Stress_ (New York: Doubleday and Co., 1979), pp. 48–51 (adapted).

10. Friedman and Ulmer, _Treating Type A Behavior,_ pp. 204–5 (adapted).

Chapter 6

1. Adapted from William Van Ornum and John B. Mordock, _Crisis Counseling with Children and Adolescents: A Guide for Non-professional Counselors_ (New York: Continuum, 1983).

2. Adapted from Carl Rogers, _A Way of Being_ (Boston: Houghton-Mifflin, 1980).

3. Van Ornum and Mordock, _Crisis Counseling with Children and Adolescents,_ pp. 37–38, 62–67 (adapted).

4. Archibald Hart, _Children and Divorce: What to Expect, How to Help_ (Waco: Word Books, 1982), pp. 124–25 (adapted).

5. Wright, _Crisis Counseling_ (see chap. 1, n. 1).

Chapter 7

1. Jay Kesler, _Parents and Teenagers_ (Wheaton, Ill.: Victor, 1984), p. 17 (adapted).

2. Ibid., pp. 151–55.

3. Dr. Keith G. Olson, _Counseling Teenagers_ (Loveland, Colo.: Group Books, 1984), pp. 27–28.

4. Ibid., pp. 55–56.

5. Fred Steit, _Parents and Problems: Through the Eyes of Youth,_ quoted in Peter H. Buntman and Eleanor M. Saris, _How to Live with Your Teenager_ (Pasadena, Calif.: Birch Tree Press, 1979), p. 14.

6. Van Ornum and Mordock, _Crisis Counseling with Children and Adolescents,_ pp. 41–43 (adapted) (see chap. 6, n. 1).

7. Frederic F. Flach and Suzanne C. Draghi, _The Nature and Treatment of Depression_ (New York: Wiley, 1975), pp. 104–6 (adapted).

8. Ibid., pp. 104–7 (adapted).

9. Olson, _Counseling Teenagers,_ pp. 495–96 (adapted).

Chapter 8

1. Smedes, *How Can It Be All Right When Everything Is All Wrong?* p. 3 (see chap. 1, n. 2).

2. Bruce Larson, *There's a Lot More to Health Than Not Being Sick* (Waco: Word Books, 1981), p. 75 (adapted).

3. Don Baker, *Pain's Hidden Purpose* (Portland, Ore.: Multnomah Press, 1984), p. 72.

4. Lloyd Ogilvie, *Why Not? Accept Christ's Healing and Wholeness* (Old Tappan, N.J.: Fleming H. Revell, 1985), p. 162.

5. "Here Comes Jesus" (author unknown).

6. Larry Richards, *When It Hurts Too Much to Wait* (Waco: Word Books, 1985), pp. 67, 68.

7. E. Borman, et al., *Interpersonal Communication in the Modern Organization* (Englewood Cliffs, N.J.: Prentice-Hall, 1969), p. 178.

8. Robert Veningo, *A Gift of Hope* (Boston: Little, Brown, and Co., 1985), p. 70 (adapted).

9. Ibid., pp. 52–82 (adapted).

10. Richards, *When It Hurts Too Much to Wait,* pp. 16, 17.

Chapter 9

1. Pat Williams and Jill Williams, with Jerry Jenkins, *Rekindled* (Old Tappan, N.J.: Fleming H. Revell, 1985), pp. 15–23. Copyright © 1985 by Fleming H. Revell Company. Published by Fleming H. Revell Company. Used by permission.

Chapter 10

1. Many of the concepts in this chapter came from Michael E. McGill, *Changing Him, Changing Her* (New York: Simon and Schuster, 1982).

Chapter 11

1. Phyllis York, David York, and Ted Wachtel, *Tough Love* (New York: Bantam Books, 1983), pp. 7–9.

2. Ibid., p. 87.

3. Ibid., pp. 95–97.

Chapter 12

1. Dr. James C. Dobson, *Love Must Be Tough* (Waco: Word Books, 1983), p. 47.

2. Ibid., pp. 147, 148 (adapted).

Bibliography

Baker, Don. *Pain's Hidden Purpose.* Portland, Ore.: Multnomah Press, 1984.

Dobson, James C. *Love Must Be Tough.* Waco, Tex: Word Books, 1983.

Freudenberger, Dr. Herbert J. *Burnout: How to Beat the High Cost of Success.* New York: Bantam Books, 1980.

Friedman, Meyer and Diane Ulmer. *Treating Type A Behavior and Your Heart.* New York: Alfred A. Knopf, 1984.

————. *Life Stress.* New York: Doubleday and Company, 1979.

Hart, Archibald. *Children and Divorce: What to Expect, How to Help.* Waco, Tex: Word Books, 1982.

Larson, Bruce. *There's a Lot More to Health Than Not Being Sick.* Waco, Tex: Word Books, 1981.

Ogilvie, Lloyd. *Why Not? Accept Christ's Healing and Wholeness.* Old Tappan, N.J.: Fleming H. Revell, 1985.

Richards, Larry. *When It Hurts Too Much to Wait.* Waco, Tex: Word Books, 1985.

Smedes, Lewis B. *How Can It Be All Right When Everything Is All Wrong?* New York: Harper and Row, 1982.

Stearns, Ann Kaiser. *Living through Personal Crisis.* New York: Ballantine Books, 1984.

Swindoll, Charles R. *Growing Strong in the Seasons of Life.* Portland, Ore: Multnomah Press, 1983.

Van Ornum, William and John B. Mordock. *Crisis Counseling with Children and Adolescents: A Guide for Non-professional Counselors.* New York: Continuum, 1983.

Veningo, Robert. *A Gift of Hope.* Boston: Little, Brown, and Co., 1985.

Welch, I. David, Donald C. Medeiros, and George A. Tate. *Beyond Burnout.* New Jersey: Prentice Hall, Inc., 1984.

Williams, Pat and Jill, with Jerry Jenkins. *Rekindled.* Old Tappan, N.J.: Fleming H. Revell, 1985.

York, Phyllis and David, and Ted Wechtel. *Tough Love.* New York: Bantam Books, 1983.

Dr. H. Norman Wright is on the faculty of Talbot Seminary in the field of Marriage and Family Counseling and is a former director of the Graduate Department of Marriage, Family, and Child Counseling at Biola University. Prior to his teaching experience he served in the local church ministry for seven years. He is the founder and director of Christian Marriage Enrichment. A licensed Marriage, Family, and Child Counselor, he maintains a private practice. He is the author of some fifty books, including *Communication—Key to Your Marriage, The Seasons of Marriage,* and *Crisis Counseling.*